collecting & restoring
WICKER FURNITURE

collecting & restoring
WICKER FURNITURE

by Richard Saunders

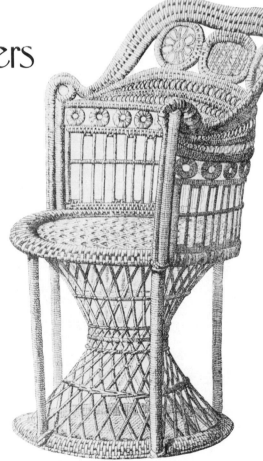

CROWN PUBLISHERS, INC.   NEW YORK

Designed by Laurie Zuckerman

Library of Congress Cataloging in Publication Data

Saunders, Richard, 1947-
    Collecting & restoring wicker furniture.

    Includes bibliographical references and index.
    1. Wicker furniture.   2.   Furniture—Repairing.
I.   Title.
TT197.7.S38   749.2'13   76-14995
ISBN: 0-517-526220

10   9   8   7   6   5

For Paula

acknowledgments

It is a pleasure to be able to express my special appreciation to Mr. Frank Stagg and Mrs. Louise Olsson for allowing me to photograph their unique collections of wicker furniture; and to Mr. William Frohmader for his expert photographic contributions.

My sincere thanks also to the efficient and courteous staffs of the Wakefield Historical Society; the Heywood-Wakefield Company; the Ohio Historical Society; the Beinecke Rare Book and Manuscript Library at Yale University; and the Sonoma County Library.

contents

collecting & restoring
WICKER FURNITURE

William Frohmader

INTRODUCTION

Within the last decade there has been a curious renaissance in the popularity of old wicker furniture in America. Although some of this wicker is accepted as genuine antique furniture, especially those pieces produced during the Victorian era, most pre-1930 wicker is considered "collectible" even if it has not yet achieved true antique status. The current revival of wicker furniture seems to have been fathered by a number of things, but it is safe to say that interior designers have played a major role by their increased use of it. Other factors that have contributed to the comeback of wicker are the nationwide trend toward nostalgia and the collecting of antiques. Also, the growing interest in crafts during the late sixties and into the seventies has renewed general interest in the craft of wickerwork, thereby leading to a true appreciation of the fine craftsmanship that went into the making of antique wicker furniture. Many young people have found that salvaging old wicker from their parents' attic or finding wicker at flea markets can result in a casual, inexpensive, and attractive way to furnish a room or a small apartment. Last, imported reproductions of fancy Victorian-style wicker furniture made recently in the Orient have aroused public interest in what the original designs really looked like.

Wicker furniture was popular in America from around the close of the Civil War to the late twenties. Then, almost overnight, it began to be considered gauche and suddenly disappeared from porches and sun rooms all across the country. Some was stowed away in attics, but much was simply consigned to the junkyard. Today wicker furniture is not only gaining in popularity daily, but most of the pre-1900 pieces have become collector's items, as have some of the better later pieces.

1

1 The rattan palm *(Calamus rotang)* grows
   wild in the East Indies. *Fairchild Tropi-
   cal Garden*

2 The rattan palm after the leaves are removed. *The Wicker Revival,* published
   by Century House

A WORD ABOUT WICKER

Before discussing the history of wicker furniture it is important first to define the term *wicker*. The word is believed to be of Scandinavian origin: from the Swedish *wika*, to bend, and *vikker*, meaning willow. Wicker is not a material in itself, as many believe, but rather a very general classification covering all woven furniture. Webster defines wicker as "a small pliant twig," but in reality wicker has evolved into an umbrella term covering such materials as rattan, cane, reed, willow, raffia, fiber, rush, and various dried grasses.

The largest amount of material used in the making of wicker furniture is derived from rattan—a climbing palm native to the East Indies (Ill. 1). There are several hundred species of rattan, all characterized by long fibrous stalks with a hard flinty coating. Actually, this plant is more like a vine than a palm, for it winds its way up neighboring trees by means of stout reversed thorns on the leaves, and attains a height of five hundred to six hundred feet without exceeding an inch and a half in diameter. Most of the rattan used for commercial purposes comes from the Far East and Southeast Asia—the finest variety, *Calamus rotang,* growing chiefly in Borneo and the Malay Archipelago, where it thrives in the jungles and swamps.

After the wild rattan is cut, the thorny leaves are removed, leaving a thin-jointed, highly polished cane that resembles young bamboo (Ill. 2). The long vines are then cut into sections, which vary in length according to the species, and are collected by traders for shipment. The rattan itself is so strong that the Orientals make rope from it that is used as cables for moorings and even for suspension bridges! Some of the species are thick enough to be used as walking canes; in fact, the word *rattan* is from the Malayan *rotan,* meaning a walking stick. The use of rattan in the making of

3

outdoor furniture has been widely accepted because of its ability to bend without breaking and its glossy, water-resistant surface.

When rattan is split, the outer bark is sliced off in long thin strips to make cane—that resilient material used in weaving openwork seats and backs for chairs. The inner bark, or pith, of rattan is called "reed." Unlike rattan, reed may be easily stained or painted any color; it is widely used in wicker furniture because of its extraordinary pliability. The reed derived from the rattan palm (not to be confused with swamp reed, which was often used in ancient wicker furniture) was first used in the manufacture of wicker furniture during the 1850s.

There are other materials used in the making of wicker furniture that are very often confused with rattan and reed. One of them is "willow." The highly pliable twigs from willow trees (sometimes called "osiers") are soft but tough, and take a good stain. "Raffia," also used in the making of wicker furniture, is a rather coarse fiber cut from the leafstalks of the raphia palm in Madagascar. "Fiber" (sometimes called "art-fiber," or "fiber-reed") came into wide use during the First World War as a new material for wicker furniture. It is made of machine-twisted paper. This material is usually soft and pliable, but some types are stiff because the paper is twisted around a flexible wire center for greater strength. To a lesser extent "rush," a perennial plant that is a member of the sedge family, and various dried grasses such as "sea grass" and "prairie grass" have also been used in the production of wicker furniture.

Although the majority of antique wicker furniture is made of rattan, reed, or willow, it is interesting to note that many pieces have been made by combining two or three of the above materials. In doing this the craftsman realized that some material lent itself better to fancy scrollwork and others to simple weaving.

EARLY WICKERWORK FURNITURE

The oldest surviving pieces of wicker furniture date back to the Egyptian empire. Because of the preserving effect of sand, the extremely dry atmosphere in that area, and the superior tombs, it is chiefly in Egypt that ancient wickerwork furniture has survived in such an excellent state after being buried for centuries. Having had a fine basketry tradition using the local palm, grasses, and rush since 4000 B.C., the ancient Egyptians gradually developed and expanded this craft until they could construct larger wickerwork items such as coffins made of coiled rush and chests made of swamp reed. Around 2000 B.C. woven reed cosmetic boxes took the place of the heavier, more elaborate chests of wood used for the same purpose. One of the finest surviving examples of this early wickerwork is a toilet chest that was found in fine condition at the burial site of Queen Menuthotep at Thebes (Ill. 3).

The Cairo Museum has a reed and papyrus chest from Thebes that was unearthed at the tomb of Yuia and Thuiu (Ill. 4). According to Mr. Hollis S. Baker, a well-known authority on ancient furniture, this chest . . .

> which is obviously an ancestor of the summer "reed furniture" of today, served a very special purpose. It contained the wigs of the lady Thuiu, who, following the custom of the day, had her head shaved for hygienic reasons; she consequently needed a suitable place to keep these important adjuncts to her wardrobe. The general construction of the chest and the wrapping of the joints between the stretchers and the legs of the chest anticipate the methods used in the making of reed and cane furniture at the present time. The little openings in the sides resemble the barred windows of a house and give the chest an architectural look—a popular device of Egyptian cabinetmakers, who often designed chests with sides resembling the facades of houses.[1]

---

[1] Hollis S. Baker, *Furniture in the Ancient World: Origins and Evolution, 3100–475 B.C.* (New York, Macmillan Company, 1966), p. 69.

3 Egyptian chest made of reed and rush (c. 1600 B.C.). *Staatliche Museum, Berlin*

4 Egyptian wig box made of reed and papyrus (c. 1400 B.C.).

5 Sumerian statue of the steward Ebih-il seated on a wicker hassock (c. 2600 B.C.). *Clichés des Musées Nationaux, Paris*

From the Sumerian civilization at Mari, in northeastern Syria, comes one of the earliest pieces of evidence attesting the existence of wicker furniture. This is a sculpture of the steward Ebih-il, sitting on a round hassock of woven reed dating back to 2600 B.C. (Ill. 5). Sumerian furniture made of reed, which was readily available from the marshes of southern Mesopotamia, was made around the same time that the first furniture appeared in Egypt. But, unlike Egyptian furniture, the remaining Early Dynastic Mesopotamian furniture consists only of a few fragments of ornamentation.

> In both cases furnishings were placed in the tombs of important persons at the time of the burials; but in Egypt the early tombs were protected by massive structures of masonry which still stand above the desert sand, whereas in Mesopotamia the tombs were constructed in a less permanent manner and the walls built of mud and brick have mostly disintegrated and disappeared from the landscape.[2]

The different climatic conditions in southern Europe account for the absence of any wickerwork relics similar to those found in the Egyptian tombs. The antiquity of wicker furniture from the Greek civilization is known only by carvings on stone, yet from the Roman Empire not only have stone carvings of wickerwork survived (Ill. 6) but written accounts from Roman authors also testify to the fact that wicker furniture was plen-

---

2 Baker, p. 159.

tiful around the time of Christ. In Rome, willows were largely cultivated for the making of baskets, chariotlike carts, and furniture. Pliny, in dealing with the cultivation of these willows and their use, wrote:

> . . . other willows throw out osiers of remarkable thinness, adapted by their suppleness and graceful slenderness for the manufacture of wicker-work. Others again, of a stouter make, are used for weaving panniers, and many other utensils employed in agriculture; while from a whiter willow the bark is peeled off, and being remarkably tractable, admits of various utensils being made of it, which require a softer and more pliable material than leather: this last is also found particularly useful in the construction of those articles of luxury, reclining chairs.[3]

The principle behind the fabrication of wickerwork furniture was simple enough: the material was woven in such a way that it was yielding and extremely comfortable to sit in because it would bend and give with the weight of the body. Thus the ancient woven chair had much in common with a piece of basketry, for it was woven in the exact same way and possessed the same qualities of lightness and flexibility.

The Roman invasions of the first century B.C. brought Britain into contact with the continent, and by the time the Romans withdrew in the fifth century A.D., the British had inherited the wicker chair. Although British traditions in wickerwork date back to the early Iron Age (through the ancient craft of basketmaking), the Britons' first contact with wickerwork furniture was through Roman wicker chairs like the one depicted in the Romano-British sepulchral monument to Julia Velva (Ill. 7). The craft of basketmaking survived the overall decay of skill that accompanied the fall of the Western Roman Empire in A.D. 476, and through its survival the scope of early British basketmaking widened to include "basket chairs" made of peeled willow twigs or woven rush. The basket chair was used by the common people throughout medieval times, but the more important members of society sat on huge wooden thrones. It is interesting to note, however, that although the design of these thrones had improved by the close of the medieval period, the simple basket chairs of the peasants were probably much more comfortable.

By the sixteenth century the wicker chair was a "people's chair" because of its low price, unpretentiousness, and immunity to changes of fashion. In 1569 the Basket Makers Guild was established in London, and it was probably from this fraternal organization that most of the wicker furniture of that period came. Unfortunately, most of its records were destroyed in the Great Fire of 1666.

An early literary reference to basket chairs (sometimes referred to as "twiggen," or "beehive," chairs) appears in the sixteenth-century work "Elegie I, on Jealosie" by John Donne:

> "Nor when he swolne, and pamper'd with great fare
> Sits downe, and snorts, cag'd in his basket chaire"

[3] Pliny *Natural History* bk. 16, chap. 68 (Bostock and Riley).

6 Stone relief showing a Roman woman seated in a wicker chair remarkably similar in design to those in use today. Early third century A.D. *Rheinisches Landesmuseum Trier*

7 A figure is shown sitting in a wicker chair at the left of this Romano-British sepulchral monument to Julia Velva. Third century A.D. *Royal Commission on Historical Monuments, England*

In sixteenth-century France the term *guérite,* meaning a sentry box, was given to a particular style of wicker armchair with an extremely high, rounded back that curved forward at the top to form a hood (Ill. 8). Probably designed for the elderly, it afforded protection against drafts and from the sunlight when used outdoors. A similar type of hooded woven "wyk-yr" chair is mentioned in English farm inventories as early as 1571. Further evidence of the hooded wicker chair can be found in a seventeenth-century painting by the Flemish artist and pupil of Rubens, Jacob Jordaens (Ill. 9).

By this time wickerwork was made around the globe. In the countries with warmer climates rattan, cane, swamp reed, various fibers, twisted palm leaves, and young bamboo were put to use, whereas the colder countries employed rush, wild grasses, willow twigs, roots, and split wood strips.

8   The French *guérite*—a sixteenth-century hooded wicker chair. *Reprinted by permission of Charles Scribner's Sons from "The Dictionary of Antiques and the Decorative Arts" compiled and edited by Louise Ade Boger. Copyright © 1957, 1967 Louise Ade Boger*

9   A wicker chair appears in this seventeenth-century painting, *The Holy Family,* by Jacob Jordaens. Note the birdcage also. *North Carolina Museum of Art*

10 The wicker cradle that came to America on the *Mayflower. Courtesy of the Pilgrim Hall Museum, Plymouth, Massachusetts*

The oldest known piece of American wickerwork came to the New World on the *Mayflower.* Legend has it that this wicker cradle (Ill. 10) was used to rock Peregrine White to sleep on the long voyage across the Atlantic. The fact that the Pilgrims came from Holland does not necessarily mean that the cradle is of Dutch origin, for the trade between China and Europe began after the establishment of a permanent settlement at Macao by the Portuguese in 1557, and it is known that Holland was actively engaged in this trade. Therefore, it is quite possible that the cradle is of Far Eastern origin.

Many American Indian tribes were expert basketmakers long before any white man came to America, yet because of their cultural differences the Indians never felt a need to produce wicker furniture. The settlers, on the other hand, brought with them the memory of simple European wicker furniture such as the straw beehive chairs of England (Ill. 11), and they were soon making their own; the proof can be found in many seventeenth-century American wills and inventories of household goods. One of the earliest of these documents, a will dated February 1639/40, comes from a certain Captain Adam Thoroughgood of Princess Anne County,

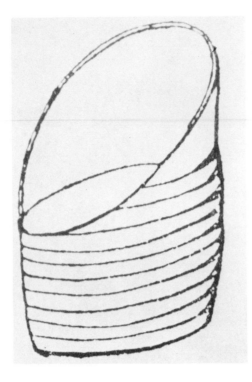

11 The straw "beehive" chair of
seventeenth- and eighteenth-
century England.

Virginia, who listed "one chair of wicker for a child" with the furniture in
Mrs. Thoroughgood's chamber.

Early in the 1660s, during the reign of Charles II, rattan was imported
into England during the beginning years of the China trade by the East
India Company. The glossy cane (the outside of rattan) was used extensively in weaving the backs and seats of wooden chairs, but the center of
the rattan was merely treated as waste. When it was first used, the cane
was wide and bulky, but by the end of the seventeenth century it was
reduced in size, and shortly thereafter chairs with very fine cane seats
were being produced in England and France.

Around the time England assumed the lead in the China trade in the
mid-eighteenth century, the Chinese, who had always closely restricted
foreign activities, decided to make Canton the one and only port for foreign trade. The wealthier Chinese merchants in Canton maintained lavish
houses, and invitations to soirées at their homes were greatly coveted by
traders of all nations. At these gatherings many British and American traders saw fanback rattan chairs in the gardens of the Chinese merchants, and
a few of these chairs made their way back to the traders' respective countries, but only as objects of curiosity or novelty items. Of far greater impor-
tance (as explained in the following chapter) was the fact that the
American traders were unwittingly bringing back a material that, at the
time, was used only to tie down the cargo but would shortly become the
building block of a giant American industry for decades to come.

THE GOLDEN AGE
OF WICKER

In the early 1840s, four new ports for foreign trade opened up in China as a result of the Opium War. By this time it was common practice for clipper ships sailing between these ports and America to carry rattan on board as dunnage to prevent the cargo from shifting. One day in 1844, while watching a vast quantity of rattan being dumped out on the docks in Boston, a young grocer named Cyrus Wakefield (Ill. 12) picked up one of the long, odd-looking poles and examined it carefully. Amazed at its flexibility, he decided to join a group of volunteers who were carting the rattan off the docks because it constituted a fire hazard. After collecting an armful of the poles, Wakefield went home and began an experiment by wrapping a provincial-style rocking chair with the discarded rattan.

Quickly realizing the great untapped potential of rattan, but having no formal training in furniture making, young Wakefield quit the grocery business and embarked on what proved to be a highly profitable jobbing trade in rattans. The demand for split rattan, or cane, for seating chairs was then increasing rapidly in America, although it had been used for this purpose in Europe as early as the seventeenth century. As luck would have it, Wakefield had a brother-in-law in the house of Messrs. Russell & Company in Canton, China, to whom he wrote and sent samples of the cane most in demand by furniture manufacturers. Wakefield knew that if he could obtain imported cane from China he would bypass the largest problem in the rattan business: that of employing workers to hand-strip the cane from whole rattan, a very slow and costly task. The correspondence proved to be successful. Within a few years he was hiring ships to bring rattan and cane back to Boston (Ill. 13), and his importations became well known throughout the United States. During these early years Wakefield also continued with his innovative experiments by designing increasingly ornate pieces of rattan furniture in the Victorian style.

12   Cyrus Wakefield I (1811–1873). *Wakefield Historical Society*

13   Wakefield clipper ship *Hoogly* discharging a cargo of rattans at Constitution Wharf, Boston. *The Five Heywood Brothers (1826–1951): A Brief History of the Heywood-Wakefield Company during 125 Years* (Richard N. Greenwood)

According to the Honorable Lilley Eaton, it was around mid-century when

> . . . a fortunate speculation gave him [Wakefield] both credit and capital, so that he could enlarge his business. Learning that there were several large lots of rattan in the New York market, the article at this time being much depressed, Mr. Wakefield, with all the ready money he could command, went to that city, established his quarters quietly at the Astor House, and put his brokers at work to obtain the lowest price at which the entire stock could be purchased, enjoining upon them not to name the purchaser. Having obtained the desired information, he decided to take all the available lots, for which he paid sufficient cash to make the material subject to his order. This gave him the whole control of the rattan stock of the country. Prices soon advanced, and he was enabled to sell, so that he realized a handsome profit. This single operation not only put money and credit at his disposal, but also gave him a prestige in the business, which he ever after maintained.[1]

Wakefield and his wife soon moved to South Reading, Massachusetts, and shortly thereafter established a rattan factory on Water Street on the Mill River. The laborers for his new factory, for which he purchased the land in 1855, were local townspeople and workers who had arrived in the Boston area in increasing numbers during and after the potato famine in

---

[1] Hon. Lilley Eaton, *Genealogical History of the Town of Reading* (Boston, Mudge, 1874), p. 680.

Ireland. By 1870 these people made up a large percentage of the labor force. Water power soon took the place of hand power, and before long steam was added as a power source to split the rattans, which were brought to South Reading from the Boston docks; the finished furniture was taken back to Boston in horse-drawn wagons. Most of Wakefield's early wicker furniture was made by combining rattan, cane (usually wrapped around a hardwood frame), and locally grown willow.

The Crystal Palace, home of London's Great Exposition of 1851, contained many pieces of the new Victorian wicker. Among them was a chair designed by John Topf of New York (Ill. 14). This is one of the earliest illustrations of American wicker furniture on record, reproduced from the "art-journal" catalog of the exposition. The chair itself received a considerable amount of attention, especially by the furniture designers of the day, who felt that the Victorian revival of the French Rococo style of the seventeenth and eighteenth centuries lent itself particularly well to the medium of wicker—motifs based on combining elaborate curves, shell forms, C-scrolls, and cabriole legs were easily and effectively adapted.

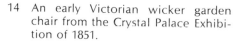

14 An early Victorian wicker garden chair from the Crystal Palace Exhibition of 1851.

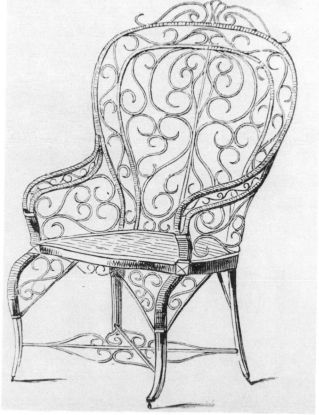

15   Wicker "sofa," armchair, rocking chair, and foot bench. Wheeler felt that the
so-called sofa, because of the pointed termination of its curves," approached
the Gothic principle of construction.

Illustrations 15 through 22 are taken from Gervase Wheeler's *Rural
Homes,* a taste manual published in New York in 1852. All this furniture
was from the warerooms of Messrs. J. & C. Berrian of New York, who
Wheeler claimed were the most extensive manufacturers of wicker furniture at that time. In the article Wheeler explained:

> . . . the wood of which the frames for the chairs, etc., are made is white oak
> or hickory, and is, in the first instance, selected with great care so that the
> grain may be straight. After being steamed to soften it, it is bent into the
> required forms and allowed to dry, so that it may not shrink or start out of
> shape after it has been made up . . . the cane itself (rattan, as it is properly
> called) is split, where it is bound on the framework—some pieces of furni-
> ture show the wood in its undivided state . . . the principal excellencies of
> cane as a material for chairs, sofas, baskets, etc., etc., are its durability, elas-
> ticity, and great facility of being turned and twisted into an almost endless
> variety of shapes; hence in chairs there is every assistance given by it in
> obtaining that greatest of all luxuries—an easy seat and a springy back.

Wheeler also mentioned that at least two thousand girls were employed
in a rattan manufactory in the Bloomingdale section of New York City, and
that the House of Refuge in New York State employed between three and
four hundred boys in the production of wicker furniture.

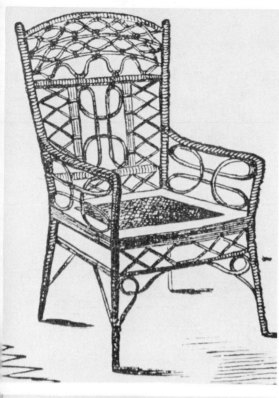

16 Sturdy wicker armchair with wrapped-cane frame, reed fancy-work, and cane seat.

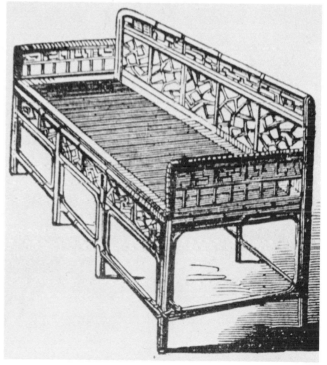

17 A wicker settee in the Chinese style made of whole rattan in such a way as to simulate the look of bamboo.

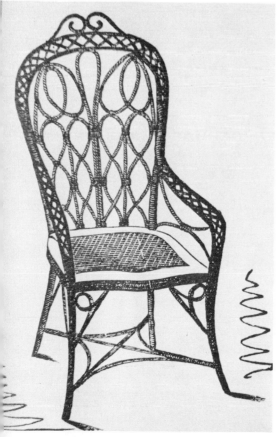

18 Lady's armchair with flowing, delicate lines.

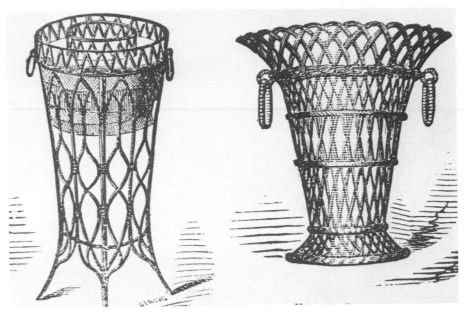

19   LEFT: Workstand for a sewing room. RIGHT: Flower stand with a metal liner for holding water or wet sand.

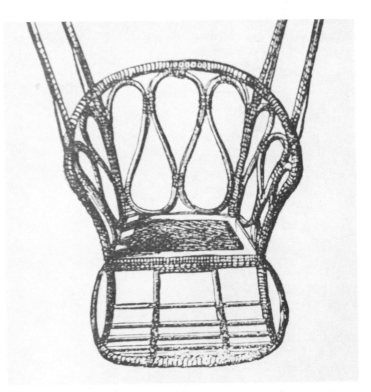

20   Unique child's swing seat with footrest and cane seat.

22 Fire screen made of rattan.

21 Wicker crib with a wrapped-cane arch as a canopy.

English wicker chairs of the mid-1850s stood in direct contrast to the ornate, flowing designs being produced in America. The basket chair developed in medieval times remained as the traditional design for wicker furniture, with few changes other than the tendency to use open-plaited skirting on the lower half of the chair (Ill. 23). A slight variation of the basket chair, which began to emerge around this time, eventually became known as the "croquet" chair. It was similar in shape to the basket chair, the major difference being its greater size. Both these chairs remained very popular in Britain throughout the nineteenth century.

23   The traditional English basket chair of the mid-1850s.

In 1856 the T'ai-p'ing Rebellion (an outgrowth of the Opium War) temporarily cut off the supply of rattan from China. Cyrus Wakefield and his assistant, an inventive Scot named William Houston, began devising methods of using the waste products of rattan already in stock and soon developed a process of spinning the shavings into a yarn from which mats were made. Through the years Houston himself produced woven floor coverings, window shades, and table mats. In 1866 he developed the first brush mat ever made of rattan, and four years later he invented a loom to weave a cane webbing that was soon to become very popular for covering seats in railroad and street-railway cars.

While Houston's weaving experiments continued, Cyrus Wakefield became obsessed with trying to find a way to use still more of the rattan, for up until this point the inner pith—called "reed"—was still treated as waste. After years of experimentation Wakefield began using the reed from rattan in the construction of frames for hoop skirts, and shortly thereafter he was using reed in the production of wicker furniture. He found it to be far more pliable than rattan and also capable of taking a good stain and paint, whereas rattan could only be lacquered.

Throughout the Civil War years furniture manufacturers realized more and more how extremely well suited wicker was to Victorian designs, and they wasted no time in capitalizing on this fact. Experimentation became all-important, and wicker furniture was pushed toward new horizons in design—horizons that seemed limitless because of the flexibility of the newly discovered reed and the relatively new and growing influence of Victorian styles in America. In fact, wicker furniture seemed like a "natural" for Victorian designs, for it combined materials (rattan, reed, cane, willow twigs, bamboo strips, and so on) just as the Victorians combined styles (Rococo, Classical, Elizabethan, Gothic, Chinese, Italian Renaissance). Between 1865 and 1880 wicker became very fashionable as porch and garden furniture, the ornate settee probably being the most popular piece of post-Civil War wicker furniture. Wicker was then used outdoors almost exclusively, although there were a few isolated cases where wicker furniture made of reed was brought inside the home and painted to match the other interior furnishings. Usually, however, wicker was left in its natural state or lightly stained and used outdoors—its advantages were its light weight and its ability to withstand the weather year-round. Many manufacturers recommended leaving dry or brittle pieces of wicker in the rain, for water restored the elastic quality so admired in this furniture.

After the war it became apparent to the citizens of South Reading that better town facilities were needed, especially a new town hall. Mr. Wakefield, by this time not only a wealthy and well-established businessman but also the town's leading citizen, rose to the occasion by donating more than $120,000 for the purpose. The local citizenry were so overcome by his generous gesture that they voted to change the name of the town to honor him, and on July 1, 1868, South Reading became Wakefield, Massachusetts.

Cyrus Wakefield's rattan business was so successful that by the early 1870s his manufactories and storehouses spanned ten acres of floorage. Then, during a financial crash known as the Panic of '73, Wakefield incorporated the Wakefield Rattan Company. He died of a heart attack just two weeks later, on October 26, 1873. Although he had large holdings in both real estate and railroad stocks, Cyrus Wakefield died bankrupt, and his widow, whose father had left a large estate, paid the deficit so that this financial condition would not appear in the town's probate records. Cyrus Wakefield II, Mr. Wakefield's nephew and namesake, returned from Singapore, where he had been since 1865 as his uncle's representative, and took over the management of the firm. In a very few years the company once again prospered.

22

24 Levi Heywood. *A Completed Century* (1926)

Shortly before his death Cyrus Wakefield had started to sell rattan to Levi Heywood (Ill. 24), founder of Heywood Brothers and Company (established in 1861). Heywood's interest in furniture making went back to 1826, when he had begun the manufacture of wooden chairs in his home town of Gardner, Massachusetts. In the 1840s Heywood devoted his attention to the construction of machinery for making furniture and invented, among other things, a combination of three machines for splitting, shaving, and otherwise manipulating rattan. One of Heywood's most remarkable inventions was a machine for bending wood, which caused Francis Thonet of Vienna (son of the creator of the famous bentwood rocker), head of the largest chair manufacturing plant in the world at that time, to write—after a visit to the Heywood factory: "I must tell you candidly that you have the best machinery for bending wood that I ever saw, and I will say that I have seen and experimented a great deal in the bending of wood."

Like Cyrus Wakefield, Levi Heywood had an inventive genius at his disposal in a certain Mr. A. Watkins. After producing several power looms that could weave cane into continuous sheets, Mr. Watkins invented an automatic channeling machine that could cut a groove around the wooden seat of a chair, thereby allowing the edges of this "sheet cane" (as it has come to be called) to be pressed into the the groove and fastened tight by means of a triangular-shaped reed called "spline." Sheet cane became extremely popular, for it was far more economical than conventional hand-caning.

By 1870 Heywood Brothers and Company, the largest chair manufacturer in the entire United States, was famous for its specialty in Windsor and bentwood chairs and the business was bringing in more than one million dollars annually. Along with various other business ventures, Heywood was one of the original stockholders of the American Rattan Company of Fitchburg, Massachusetts, one of the oldest rattan companies in America. Around 1875 Cyrus Wakefield II bought out several small competitors in the rattan industry, among them the American Rattan Company, and shortly thereafter Levi Heywood began the manufacture of wicker furniture himself.

In 1876 the Philadelphia Centennial Exhibition featured an international display of the finest arts and crafts of the day. Among the most notable pieces of wicker furniture were the "hourglass" chairs from China (Ill. 25), probably the last quality wicker furniture to be made for the West. These chairs became so popular in America within the next few years that they were not only imported in quantity but widely imitated by American manufacturers.

The Wakefield Rattan Company, having recently expanded to the West Coast by establishing a branch office in San Francisco, entered the exhibition and received an award "for original design and superior workmanship in furniture, chairs, and baskets, also for originality in the manufacture of mats and baskets of an otherwise waste material; also for a new form of car seats, durable, cool, clean, and economical."[2] As to the "new form of car seats" mentioned above, Richard N. Greenwood, a great grandson of Levi Heywood and president of the Heywood-Wakefield Company from 1929 to 1966, reminds us that, several years before Philadelphia's Centennial Exhibition, William Houston of the Wakefield Rattan Company

> developed ingenious looms for weaving the cane into a fabric. It was this machinery and skill in weaving long, continuous sheets of cane webbing that put the Wakefield Rattan Company into the railway and street car seating business, for cane was then acknowledged as the best material with which to cover seats of this type.[3]

In the late 1870s wicker chairs from Ceylon with retractable footrests and wide arms (Ill. 26) caught the attention of one British writer, who said of them:

> It seems a pity that sofas and chairs made of straw or bamboo should not be more used than they are. I mean, used as they come from the maker's hands, not painted or gilded, and becushioned and bedizened into hopeless vulgarity. They are only admissible "au naturel," and should stand upon their own merits.[4]

Although most wicker furniture at this time was still left in its natural state, there was a growing tendency on the part of the general public to paint wicker, and by the 1880s, when reed had replaced rattan as the material most commonly used in the production of wicker furniture, manufacturers came to realize that the buying public preferred reed furniture because it could take paint and therefore be moved indoors. Plants, along with the sunlight, had invaded the Victorian sitting room, and wicker plant stands were suddenly in great demand. The production of rattan-made furniture, with its shiny surface that resisted all stains and paint, was quickly dying.

[2] Francis A. Walker, ed., *International Exhibition; Reports and Awards*, vol. 4 (Washington, Government Printing Office, 1880), p. 738.
[3] Richard N. Greenwood, *The Five Heywood Brothers (1826–1951): A Brief History of the Heywood-Wakefield Company During 125 Years* (New York, Newcomen Publications, 1951), p. 16.
[4] Lady Barker, *The Bedroom and Boudoir* (London, Macmillan and Company, 1878), pp. 80–82.

25   An hourglass wicker chair in the Chinese style similar to those at the Philadelphia Centennial Exhibition of 1876. The chair was named after the hourglass design below the seat.

26   A slant-back wicker chair with retractable footrest from Ceylon (c. 1870). This type of lightweight chair was in common use aboard passenger ships of the period. The frame was made of bamboo; the material used in the weaving was cane. The wide armrests were often put to good use to hold food and drink. This style of chair was also on display in the Chinese pavilion at the Philadephia Centennial Exhibition of 1876.

During the 1870s Levi Heywood developed a new method of bending rattan to greater extents. This method, adapted from his own experiments in wood bending, encouraged the wicker furniture manufacturers of the day to experiment with new designs using graceful rattan frames around which narrow strips of flat reed or cane were wrapped. When this new method of bending rattan was coupled with the dramatic fancywork made possible through the use of the elastic-like reed, the results were truly fantastic—but better than a description in words, let's look through some sample pages from the 1881 Wakefield Rattan Company catalog (Ills. 27–31).

27 Children's wicker from the 1881 Wakefield Rattan Company catalog: rocker with openwork back; rocker with spider-web caned back; rare potty chairs. *The Beinecke Rare Book and Manuscript Library, Yale University*

28 LEFT: The lady's diamond-panel rocker was one of the most popular wicker designs of the Victorian era. RIGHT: The gentleman's version of the same rocker is slightly larger and has diamond-shaped panels under the arms. *The Beinecke Rare Book and Manuscript Library, Yale University*

STAR BACK PATTERN.
No. 437. Conversation. $20.00

EXTRA RING HIGH BACK PATTERN.
No. 143. Tete-a-tete. Length of seat, 3 ft. 3 in., $20.00

29   Victorian conversation chair with spider-web caned back and caned seats.
*The Beinecke Rare Book and Manu-
script Library, Yale University*

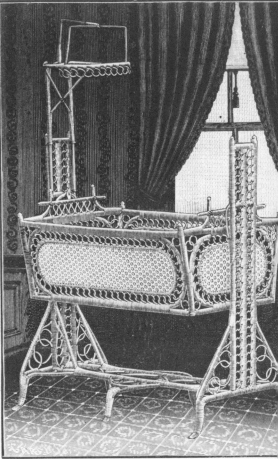

No. 428. Star Panel Swing Crib, $19.00
With Canopy, 20.00

30   Ornate settee from the Wakefield Rattan Company
catalog of 1881. *The Beinecke Rare Book and Manuscript Library, Yale University*

31   Elaborate Victorian swinging crib. Very
rare. *The Beinecke Rare Book and Manuscript Library, Yale University*

Although the manufacture of wicker baby carriages (also known as perambulators) began during the Civil War, there was little demand for them until the mid-1870s, when Heywood Brothers and Company began turning out quality carriages in large numbers. By the 1880s wicker baby carriages had become so popular that Levi Heywood's company began printing separate trade catalogs for these unique vehicles. The illustrations reproduced here (Ills. 32–36) are from the 1886 Heywood Brothers and Company baby carriage catalog.

32 Reed baby carriage with parasol; Victorian. The body, which resembles an upturned seashell, was stained cherry and varnished at the factory. *Ohio Historical Society*

33 Victorian hooded baby carriage with an enameled cane body. The upholstery was usually silk or satin, the standard colors being cardinal, wine, gold, light blue, peacock, or brown. *Ohio Historical Society*

34 An extremely ornate Victorian reed carriage with fancy scrollwork. Reed body, stained cherry, is varnished. *Ohio Historical Society*

35 Twin carriages made of reed and stained cherry, as this one is, were produced in limited quantities in the 1880s, and so are understandably rare today. Most carriages then had elliptic front and back springs. *Ohio Historical Society*

36 A hooded reed carriage with runners for winter use! Virtually all the Heywood Brothers baby carriages of this period could be converted into sleighs, like the one at left, simply by removing the wheels and putting on runners, which were sold separately by the company. *Ohio Historical Society*

In America the 1880s was perhaps the most important decade in wicker furniture design, for the experiments of the preceding two decades had now been fully developed and perfected by highly skilled craftsmen. It is interesting to note here that some of the styles developed as far back as the Civil War were still in use during the eighties. Hence, the modern-day practice of dating wicker furniture by style alone is not as reliable as it might seem.

The public finally accepted wicker on a large scale once it was realized that the three-dimensional, airy quality of this furniture was equally suited to the garden, the porch, and the sitting room. As the popularity of wicker continued to grow, many new companies were established with the idea of cashing in on what was thought to be a nationwide trend. Well-established furniture manufacturers also began to include wicker in their showrooms, and by the late 1880s both Sears, Roebuck and Company and Montgomery Ward Company offered reed and rattan furniture at greatly reduced prices, although the workmanship and quality of the materials in their furniture were inferior to those of the pieces produced by older firms specializing in wicker furniture. Almost all the reed furniture of the period was varnished or stained at the factories, in order to seal the porous material and at the same time give it a more finished look, but the public's penchant for painting wicker was stronger than ever. Countless pieces were painted white, dark green, brown, and—in some extreme cases—gold!

For the Wakefield Rattan Company and Heywood Brothers and Company, this decade was one of keen competition; as Richard N. Greenwood said in his speech commemorating the 125th anniversary of the Heywood Brothers furniture business: "Both firms grew at about the same rate, both were being managed by first or second generations, and both were making related products during the last quarter of the century."[5] Moreover, both companies suffered painful setbacks during the eighties. One of the main buildings of the Wakefield Rattan Company burned to the ground in 1881 and had to be completely rebuilt (Ill. 37), and in 1888 Cyrus Wakefield II died, leaving the management of his company to relatively inexperienced men who had been in the organization with him but had little practical experience in running a business. In 1882 the firm of Heywood Brothers and Company suffered the loss of their founder, Levi Heywood, and Henry Heywood (Levi's nephew) was chosen to carry on the business. Yet both companies survived these setbacks and continued their industrial rivalry. Again, in the same commemorative speech, Mr. Greenwood told an amusing story that illustrated this rivalry between the two firms around 1883:

> Both wanted a Chicago plant and warehouse. In spite of their competing interests, they decided to establish a joint manufacturing enterprise there. Representatives of both firms met in Chicago for the purpose of finding a suitable building. The first day's search was fruitless, so it was decided to renew the quest the following day. The next morning, however, the Wake-

[5] Greenwood, p. 17.

field men left early, found a plant and informed the Heywood representatives that the building was so satisfactory that they would purchase it independently and operate it themselves. After the resulting storm subsided, Henry Heywood and Amos Morrill of Heywood Brothers and Company found a plant to their liking, which was to be the Chicago factory and warehouse until 1930. It is safe to assume that competition was keener than ever during the years following this Chicago episode.[6]

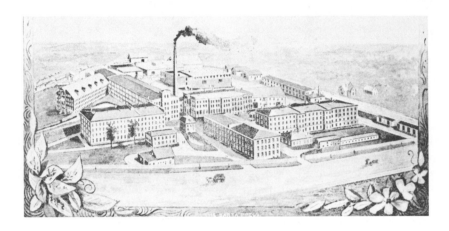

WAKEFIELD RATTAN CO.

Importers of Rattan and Manufacturers of Rattan and Reed Furniture ; Cane and Wood Seat Chairs ; Children's Carriages
Chair Cane ; Car Seats, etc., etc.

SALESROOMS :—Boston, New York, Chicago, San Francisco.   FACTORIES :—Wakefield, Chicago, Kankakee, Ill., San Francisco.

37   After the fire of 1881, the main building of the Wakefield Rattan Company was rebuilt with brick. This print shows the Wakefield plant in the early 1890s. *Wakefield Historical Society*

In February of 1897 the Wakefield Rattan Company merged with the firm of Heywood Brothers and Company to form a new organization—"Heywood Brothers and Wakefield Company." Henry Heywood, head of the new company, saw the consolidation of the two great companies as a kind of pooling of resources, and immediately began to employ Wakefield's cane-weaving machinery to produce cane seat coverings for electric streetcars as well as entire railroad seats. Of course, the main interest of the new company was still the manufacture of wicker furniture, and one of Henry Heywood's first acts as president of the Heywood Brothers and Wakefield Company was to establish warehouses in London and Liverpool, England. Wicker furniture was still very popular in turn-of-the-century America, but the winds of change were beginning to gust.

Here are selected illustrations (Ills. 38–45) from the 1899 Heywood Brothers and Wakefield Company catalog, the third joint catalog put out by the newly formed company. A collection of photographs of Victorian wicker furniture (Ills. 46–71) follows immediately thereafter.

---

[6] Greenwood, pp. 17–18.

6315 B. P. R.
LADY'S COMFORT PATENT ROCKER.
Fancy Colored Reeds.

6317 B. P. R.
LADY'S COMFORT PATENT ROCKER.

6315 D. P. R.
LARGE COMFORT PATENT ROCKER.
Fancy Colored Reeds.

6317 D. P. R.
LARGE COMFORT PATENT ROCKER.

38   Various styles of platform rockers. All four of the examples
shown here have hollow serpentine arms and backs. *Wakefield
Historical Society*

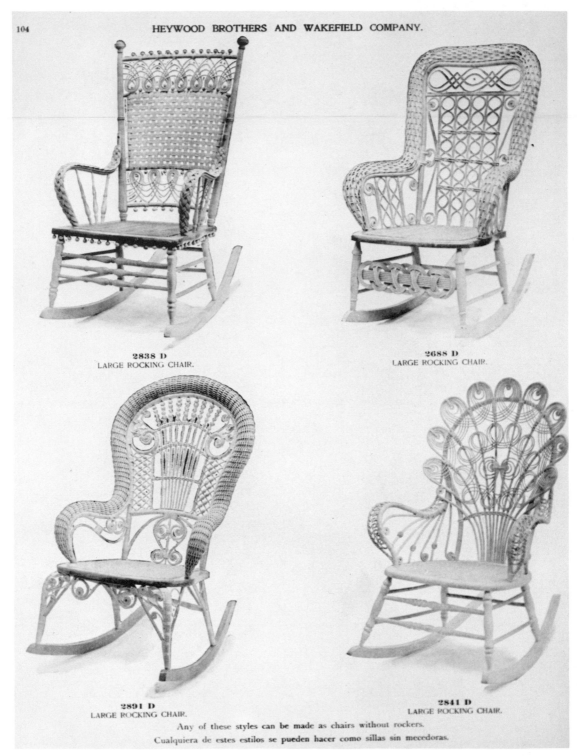

104   HEYWOOD BROTHERS AND WAKEFIELD COMPANY.

2838 D
LARGE ROCKING CHAIR.

2688 D
LARGE ROCKING CHAIR.

2891 D
LARGE ROCKING CHAIR.

2841 D
LARGE ROCKING CHAIR.

Any of these styles can be made as chairs without rockers.
Cualquiera de estes estilos se pueden hacer como sillas sin mecedoras.

39   Four rockers of vastly different designs, yet they have one thing
in common: caned seats. *Wakefield Historical Society*

HEYWOOD BROTHERS AND WAKEFIELD COMPANY.   131

6259

CONVERSATION CHAIR.

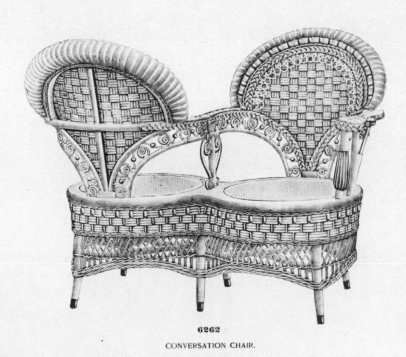

6262

CONVERSATION CHAIR.

40   Two styles of the popular conversation chair. These chairs became the love seats of the Victorian era because a respectable couple could sit next to each other without touching. *Wakefield Historical Society*

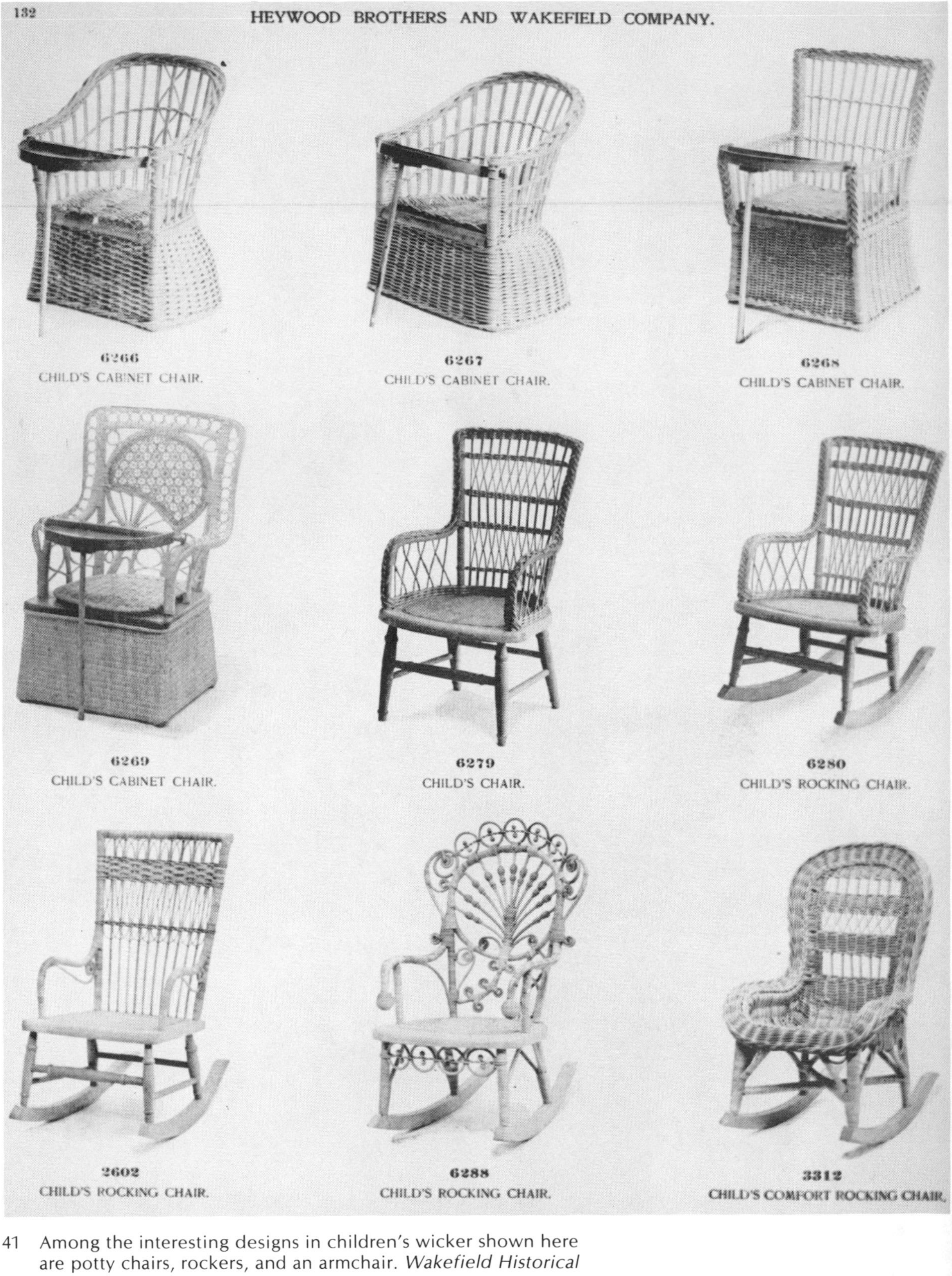

132

HEYWOOD BROTHERS AND WAKEFIELD COMPANY.

6266
CHILD'S CABINET CHAIR.

6267
CHILD'S CABINET CHAIR.

6268
CHILD'S CABINET CHAIR.

6269
CHILD'S CABINET CHAIR.

6279
CHILD'S CHAIR.

6280
CHILD'S ROCKING CHAIR.

2602
CHILD'S ROCKING CHAIR.

6288
CHILD'S ROCKING CHAIR.

3312
CHILD'S COMFORT ROCKING CHAIR.

41   Among the interesting designs in children's wicker shown here
are potty chairs, rockers, and an armchair. *Wakefield Historical
Society*

42 A mixed group of wicker furniture. LEFT: A relative of the sixteenth-century French *guérite* hooded wicker chair; this 1899
version has a caned seat and side windows. CENTER: Elaborate
dressing stand complete with beveled mirror. RIGHT: Cabinet
with five shelves. *Wakefield Historical Society*

HEYWOOD BROTHERS AND WAKEFIELD COMPANY.

6264
BEACH CHAIR.
66 inches High.

6445
DRESSING STAND.
Top, 18 x 29 inches.

6444
FANCY CABINET.
28 x 60 Inches.

159

HEYWOOD BROTHERS AND WAKEFIELD COMPANY.

889
BOOK CASE.

891
EASEL.

3976
EASEL.
76 inches High.

894
EASEL.
72 inches High.

43 Extremely ornate bookcase and three wicker easels, all of which
are rare pieces of the sort eagerly sought by the collector.
Wakefield Historical Society

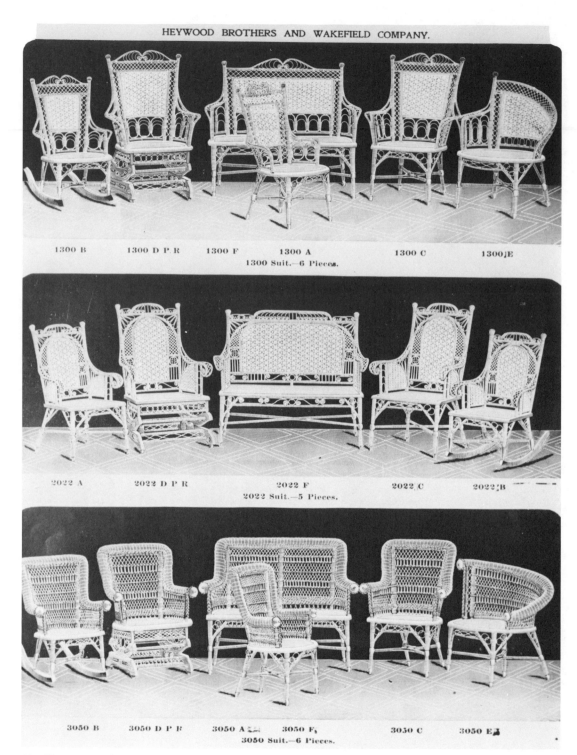

HEYWOOD BROTHERS AND WAKEFIELD COMPANY.

1300 B   1300 D P R   1300 F   1300 A   1300 C   1300 E
1300 Suit.—6 Pieces.

2022 A   2022 D P R   2022 F   2022 C   2022 B
2022 Suit.—5 Pieces.

3050 B   3050 D P R   3050 A   3050 F   3050 C   3050 E
3050 Suit.—6 Pieces.

44   Three complete sets of matching wicker furniture. *Wakefield Historical Society*

172   HEYWOOD BROTHERS AND WAKEFIELD COMPANY.

3710 E   3710 C   3710 F   3710 A   3710 D P R   3710 B
3710 Suit.—6 Pieces.

4170 B, K D   4170 C, K D   4170 F, K D   4170 D, K D   4170 A, K D
4170 K D Suit. 5 Pieces.

4169 B, K D   4169 C, K D   4169 F, K D   4169 D, K D   4169 A, K D
4169 K D Suit.—5 Pieces.

45   Three matching sets of wicker. *Wakefield Historical Society*

46   Two rockers with unique back panels. LEFT: This one-of-a-kind
     rocker is a true museum piece. The leather cameo panel set into
     the back is framed by wicker braiding. *Frank Stagg.* RIGHT: A
     gentleman's rocker with a pressed-oak back panel and oak spools.
     Mike York

47   A rare find—a three-piece set of natural wicker in mint condition.
     Both settee and matching armchairs have open horseshoe designs
     worked into their tightly woven backs. *Frank Stagg*

48 Various styles of Victorian rockers. TOP LEFT: Natural serpentine rocker. *Frank Stagg.* TOP RIGHT: Lady's rocker with spider-web caning in the back. *John Hathaway.* BOTTOM LEFT: High-backed rocker. *Beverly Stephenson.* BOTTOM RIGHT: Gentleman's rocker with wooden spools and serpentine arms and back. *John Hathaway*

49   Victorian rockers. TOP LEFT: The thick wicker braiding on this rocker forms graceful lines. TOP RIGHT: An old peacock design, which is commonly reproduced today. BOTTOM LEFT: Ornate rocker from the 1880s. BOTTOM RIGHT: These thick serpentine rolled arms are unique because they continue down to the bottom of the piece and actually frame the entire rocker. *Frank Stagg (all photos)*

50 TOP LEFT: Platform rocker from the 1890s. TOP RIGHT: Natural rocker with ornate spoolwork and curlicues in the back. *Beverly Stephenson.* BOTTOM LEFT: Serpentine rocker. BOTTOM RIGHT: Gentleman's rocker with caned seat.

51 Three types of Victorian chairs. TOP: Conversation chair. BOTTOM LEFT: Corner chair with elaborate use of spools and curlicues. *Frank Stagg.* BOTTOM RIGHT: Straight-back chair with butterfly design worked into the back.

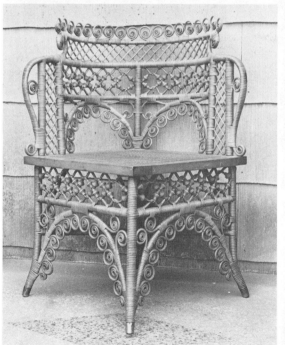

52 The three corner chairs shown here are typical of those used as props in most photography studios of the late 1800s. TOP: Large corner chairs like this one were sometimes called bustle benches. Note the heart-shaped back. BOTTOM LEFT: Ornate corner chair. BOTTOM RIGHT: Corner chair with serpentine back. *Frank Staff (all photos)*

53   TOP: Straight-back chair. *John Hathaway*. BOTTOM LEFT: Very ornate armchair with woven seat of reeds. *Frank Stagg*. BOTTOM RIGHT: This heart-shaped Victorian design is one of the most widely reproduced wicker designs of modern times. *Frank Stagg*

54 TOP LEFT: Lady's armchair. *Frank Stagg.* TOP RIGHT: Rare wicker Morris chair reclines for greater comfort. *Frank Stagg.* BOTTOM LEFT: Corner chair literally dripping with curlicues. *Frank Stagg.* BOTTOM RIGHT: Armchair with Japanese fan design worked into the back.

55 Various styles of Victorian wicker settees. TOP LEFT: Serpentine settee with spider-web caning set into the back. TOP RIGHT: Ornate settee with wooden spools set into the back. *Frank Stagg.* BOTTOM LEFT: Settee with fancywork back and caned seat. *Frank Stagg.* BOTTOM RIGHT: Tightly woven settee. *Frank Stagg*

56 Two whatnots. LEFT: Small case with three oak shelves. RIGHT: Seven-foot whatnot with elaborate scrollwork. *Frank Stagg (both pieces)*

57 Two styles of bedside tables. *Frank Stagg*

58   Tables from the Victorian era. TOP LEFT: Small table with extra shelf. *Frank Stagg.* TOP RIGHT: Large square table with cane-matted top and 104 curlicues. BOTTOM LEFT: Large table with birdcage design in center. *Frank Stagg.* BOTTOM RIGHT: Natural table with inlaid wood top and serpentine sides. *Frank Stagg*

59 Three styles of sewing baskets, all from around 1880. *Beverly Stephenson (bottom right)*

60   Three types of wicker music stands. TOP: Small, openwork stand with ball feet. *Frank Stagg.* BOTTOM LEFT: Classic music stand from the 1880s. *Alice M. Saare.* BOTTOM RIGHT: Elaborate stand with three oak shelves. *Frank Stagg*

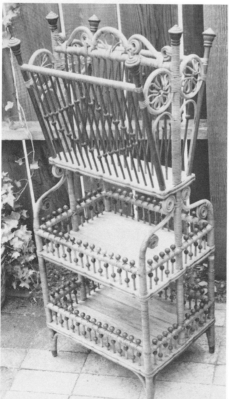

61 Victorian children's wicker. TOP: Ornate buggy with caned bottom, adjustable back, and silk umbrella. BOTTOM LEFT: High chair. BOTTOM RIGHT: Child's stroller with adjustable footrest. *Carol Wrathall*

62 TOP: Upholstered lounge from 1890s. *Frank Stagg.*
    BOTTOM: Wicker couch or daybed.

63 Rare organ stool with serpentine back and birdcage legs. *Frank Stagg*

64 Pie caddy. *Frank Stagg*

65 Smoking stand with metal insert attached on the top for striking matches. *Frank Stagg*

66   Vanity bench. *Frank Stagg*

67   Umbrella rack. *Frank Stagg*

68   Rare wicker wheelchair, or "phaeton." *Frank Stagg*

69 Small table with marble top. *Frank Stagg*

70 Elaborate wicker buffet. *Frank Stagg*

71 Wicker picture frame. *Nadine Smedshammer*

72 A typical "outdoor" room furnished with wicker.

THE TURN OF THE CENTURY

Around the turn of the century a number of great changes occurred. Not only did the automobile take the place of the horse car but the home use of electricity and central heating became widespread. As a result of the new hot-air heating systems, porches were glassed in to create comfortable sun parlors with an airy feel to them. Wicker furniture was almost always used to furnish these "family," or "outdoor," rooms, as they were sometimes called (III. 72).

The manufacturers of this furniture, in keeping up with the demand, began to design a far greater number of matching chairs, tables, lounges, and settees—that is, complete "sets" of wicker furniture. In the past, the majority of wicker pieces had been more individual in style and just one or two were used to add variety to a room or give a more casual atmosphere.

From the standpoint of the design of American wicker furniture, the turn-of-the-century period relied heavily on the earlier Victorian styles with very little experimentation. The Art Nouveau style, which did not appear on the American scene until the 1890s, was easily adapted to wicker furniture, but relatively few Art Nouveau wicker pieces were produced during this period simply because the Victorian styles in wicker furniture were still popular.

According to the Wakefield Historical Society, the labor force at Heywood Brothers and Wakefield Company changed radically after 1900: many of the rattan factory workers were now of Italian extraction. The reason behind this shift from Irish to Italian workers was twofold. First, as a result of the poor economic conditions in Italy, many Italian men came to the Wakefield area to work on the construction of public utilities and other construction jobs. When these projects were completed, some of the men found jobs in the rattan factory and then sent for their families to come from Italy and join them in Wakefield. Second, by the early 1900s many of the next generation Irish, whose parents and grandparents had worked for the Wakefield Rattan Company since its inception in the mid-1840s, had found different occupations, and therefore there were many employment openings at Heywood Brothers and Wakefield Company.

During the early 1900s, wicker furniture from the Far East was still being imported into many countries. The hourglass chair from Canton, China, which had become extremely popular in America after the Philadelphia Centennial Exhibition of 1876, became known as the Canton chair, and before long the Chinese were exporting complete matching sets in what was generally known as the hourglass design (Ill. 73). A. A. Vantine and Company of New York had imported this furniture direct from Canton since 1900, and their advertisements boasted of its graceful design and inexpensiveness, as well as pointed out that each piece was "woven by hand, without a nail in [its] entire construction." This Oriental wicker was lighter than its American counterpart because the framework was made of bamboo rather than heavier wood. Reed and rattan were woven over the bamboo frame, and in most cases the chairs had canework backs and seats. Even to this day there is a widespread misconception among the general public that most antique wicker is from the Orient, yet the truth of the matter is that the majority of pre-1920 wicker pieces were made in America.

In Europe (as in America, but to a far lesser extent), the trend in wicker furniture was toward angular rather than flowing designs. A handful of Austrian architects began designing more conservative, straight-lined furniture, and they often made use of cushions and plush upholstery (Ill. 74). In their use of overstuffed seats and upholstery many of these architect-designers seemed to disregard the basic principle on which wicker furniture had first been constructed thousands of years earlier—that woven furniture holds much the same qualities of intimacy and charm as a piece of basketry in that it is woven in the same way and therefore shares the same elastic-like spring and flexibility! Furthermore, even the unupholstered angular designs seemed far more rigid because of the wide, flat seats (Ill. 75), and therefore stood in direct contrast to most Victorian wicker furniture, which utilized slightly concave seats and backs in order to better fit the human body and "give" when in use.

It is interesting to note that the material used in making the Austrian wicker of this period was grown in a special plot of land in the famous Vienna Prater entirely given up to the culture of different species of the willow. The wicker furniture made of these peeled osiers was an ivory white that gradually, through the years, turned to a soft golden tone.

The English wicker of this period, called "cane furniture" by the British, was made from willows grown in Somerset and the Thames Valley. Experiments carried out at the Leicester Art School by B. J. Fletcher and Charles Crampton culminated in the birth of the Dryad Works in 1907. The early designs developed at the Dryad Works by Charles and Albert Crampton, members of an old British basketmaking family, were not as rigid looking as the Austrian furniture, but emphasized curving, circular designs with

73 A matching set of hourglass wicker furniture from the Far East (c. 1900). The chair on the left, called the Hong Kong club chair, was probably meant as a lady's chair to be used alongside the ever popular Canton chair *(right)* The table in the middle is also of the hourglass design and therefore very stable because of its large base. The oil lamp is also made of reed and rattan.

74 An Austrian-made upholstered wicker armchair from the early 1900s. The angular construction marked a return to basic design as well as a revolt against the overly ornate Victorian wicker designs that were still being produced in America.

75 A turn-of-the-century Austrian design shows the rigidity of the flat, unyielding seat as opposed to earlier Victorian designs that stressed flexibility. However, the slanted backrest on this particular chair is a unique feature in wicker furniture and does give the appearance of having a somewhat elastic quality.

"Dryad" English Cane Furniture

THIS delightful and practical style of Summer Furniture is new to America, but is widely identified with country home life in England to-day. It finds its highest expression in the attractive and graceful Cane Chairs, Settees, Tables, Tea Waggons, Flower Stands, Dog Baskets, etc., displayed in our Division of Furniture and Decoration.

"DRYAD" Cane Furniture is without equal for use on porches and lawns. It possesses also the artistic character, substantial construction and comfortable qualities, which adapt it as well to year-round use indoors.

"DRYAD" Cane Furniture is made of the strongest unbleached pulp cane without the use of nails or tacks. The frames are of best quality ash. This construction is vastly superior to that usually found in ordinary willow, reed and rattan furniture.

The smooth finish and skillful shaping of the different models provide comfort without the necessity of cushions.

Imported and sold exclusively by us in New York and vicinity. The genuine identified by this metal label; [DRYAD FURNITURE LEICESTER ENGLAND]

Illustrated Catalogue "The 'DRYAD' Cane Book" will be mailed upon request

W. & J. SLOANE

Interior Decorators   Furniture Makers
Floor Coverings and Fabrics
FIFTH AVENUE AND FORTY-SEVENTH STREET, NEW YORK

76 A 1914 magazine advertisement for Dryad English cane furniture.

full-length skirting on major pieces such as chairs and settees. Aside from being very popular in England, Dryad furniture was also imported by W. & J. Sloane of New York (Ill. 76).

By 1910 a shift in American taste toward simplicity and away from Victorian-style wicker became quite evident, and in less than a decade Victorian and Art Nouveau designs were totally rejected and considered gauche. In an overreaction against such flowing designs people carted the elaborate pieces off to the dump or, at best, found a place for them in the attic. Although some Victorian designs were still lingering in 1915, they were forced to share the spotlight with the new and sobering influence of the angular, straight-lined Mission style—as can be seen in two pages (ills. 77–78) from the Sears, Roebuck and Company catalog of 1915.

Reed Furniture

Popular Reed Rocker

Only
$2.99

This is the most popular Reed Rocker we have ever sold. It is made of imported reeds, finished in shellac over a thoroughly seasoned frame of maple, doweled and glued, insuring a very rigid and substantial rocker. Has a wide, roomy seat, comfortable roll arms and high back, together with a perfect rest giving quality not usually found in other rockers at a much higher price. Shipping weight, about 14 pounds.

No. 1D910
Price,
$2.99

Because of the rounding curved lines, and the suppleness and flexibility of the reeds, reed furniture is exceptionally comfortable. Another reason for its popularity is its lightness, making it very easy to handle and move about. There is a great difference in the various makes of reed furniture, and extreme care should be taken in its selection. All our rockers and settees are made of an excellent quality of imported reeds. The frames are carefully constructed of seasoned Northern hardwood and are made of stock of ample size to insure perfect strength. The posts and cross stretchers are carefully fitted, securely fastened, making a solid, strong and rigid piece. The imported reeds are tough, flexible fibers, and will not break or split. They are closely woven by hand by highly skilled workmen. The finish is very carefully applied and is very durable.

NO HOME is complete without at least one or two reed rockers, and you will find a very wide selection on this and the next page. We make you a big saving in price because of our direct method of merchandising. You do not have to pay the big profits of a long chain of jobbers, dealers, retailers, etc., when you buy from us. Buying in enormous quantities to supply our many thousands of customers, we are able to secure from the manufacturers the lowest possible prices. These benefits are in turn given to our customers. Our prices speak for themselves. We welcome the closest comparison.

Cane Seat Reed Rocker

Only
$3.28

A choice unique design that will fit well into almost every home, no matter what the other furnishings may be. Made of an excellent quality imported reeds, shellac finish, woven over a thoroughly seasoned frame of maple. Very strong and rigid. A heavy continuous closely woven roll entirely surrounding back, arms and seat. Beneath the seat is a medium size reed skirt. The roomy, comfortable seat is covered with a fine quality of closely woven cane. Would command a much higher price elsewhere. Shipping wt., about 15 pounds.
No. 1D919
Price,
$3.28

Remarkably Good Values—Remarkably Good Rockers.

Price,
$2.43

No. 1D903 A popular pattern at a remarkably low price. Made with flat continuous arms and closely woven back. The frame is made of thoroughly seasoned hardwood. Excellent quality reeds. Finished in natural shellac. Broad roomy seat. Roll front. Strong, rigid and durable. A splendid value. Shipping wt., about 13 pounds.

Price,
$2.68

No. 1D905 Large Comfortable Reed Rocker, has extra high back and wide seat, closely woven with double strand reeds. Has full continuous roll around back and arms. The frame is made of thoroughly seasoned hardwood, natural shellac finish. This rocker is firmly constructed and a wonderfully good value at our low price. Shipping weight, about 12 pounds.

Price,
$3.78

No. 1D924 Thin Women's Reed Rocker only $3.78. The reeds are an excellent imported stock. Extra wide back with continuous roll arms extending under seat and supported by scrolls. Wide seat covered with fine cane, and almost solid reed back. Solidly constructed frame of seasoned hardwood, natural finish. An excellent value at our low price. Shipping weight, about 17 pounds.

Price,
$3.86

No. 1D927 Large Size Reed Rocker, one of the latest designs. Constructed with a view to comfort and durability. It has a wide roll seat, full wrapped continuous arms and posts, and is made over a maple frame, thoroughly seasoned. Carefully wrapped and packed and safe delivery guaranteed. Shipping weight, about 15 pounds.

Price,
$3.98

No. 1D935 Handsome Cane Seat Reed Rocker, exceptionally well made. Has low back with beautiful heavy roll extending from back over the arms to seat. Frame is family braced underneath seat. Natural shellac finish. It is one of the most popular styles and is an exceptional value at the price we ask. Shipping weight, about 14 pounds.

Price,
$3.97

No. 1D931 Extra Wide Back Comfortable Rocker, made of an excellent quality of imported reeds over a thoroughly seasoned hardwood frame. Wide, continuous roll is closely woven and extends entirely around back and arms. This is a big roomy rocker having unusual comfort giving qualities. Shipping weight, about 15 pounds.

Price,
$4.24

No. 1D938 Combination Nurse's or Sewing Rocker. A comfortable practical rocker for women's use. Has low arm rests, a medium high back and basket at the side for holding sewing material or other articles. Frame is seasoned maple, doweled and firmly glued. The reed work is all of imported stock finished golden brown. Shipping weight, about 14 pounds.

Price,
$4.68

No. 1D941 Made of selected imported reeds over a thoroughly seasoned hardwood frame. Natural shellac finish. Large, roomy seat with roll front and a continuous roll extending over back and arms. This is a broad, spacious, restful rocker that will make any room in your home vastly more inviting and comfortable. Shipping weight, about 16 pounds.

Price,
$5.98

No. 1D944 Large Comfortable Reed Rocker. Made of selected imported reeds over a thoroughly seasoned maple frame. Finished in natural shellac. Has wide roomy seat and high back. The heavy continuous roll is closely woven and extends entirely around the back over arms and front posts. A big, high grade rocker that will give good service. Shipping wt., about 17 lbs.

Price,
$6.18

No. 1D935 This Rocker is built with a comfortable spring seat, padded back and has the low arms. Has extra roomy basket on side for sewing materials or other articles. The frame is made of seasoned maple. The seat is 17x19 inches. The reeds are all imported and are finished in the golden brown finish. Has beautifully figured cretonne back and seat cushions. Shipping weight, about 17 pounds.

77 Page from the 1915 Sears, Roebuck and Company catalog. *Sears, Roebuck and Co.*

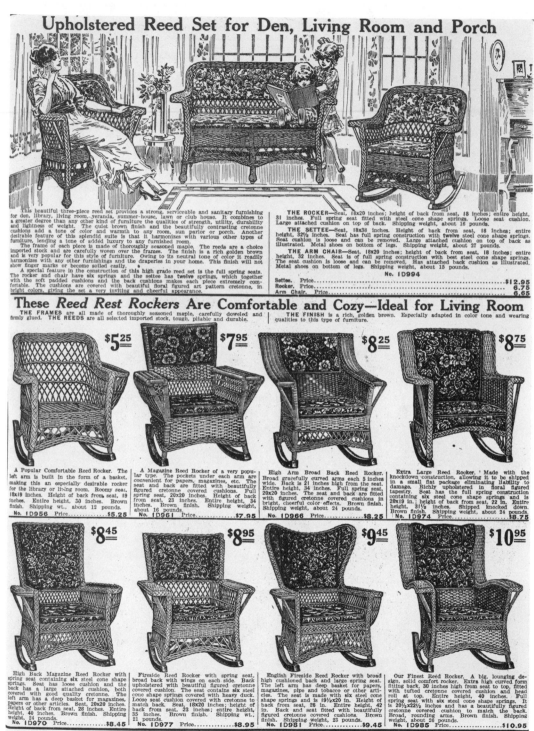

78   Page from the 1915 Sears, Roebuck and Company catalog. *Sears, Roebuck and Co.*

Not only had wicker made the transition from outdoor to indoor furniture, as the following excerpts from a popular magazine of the day will attest; it had also gained the acceptance of leading decorators such as James Collier Marshall, whose article "Among the Wicker Shops" appeared in *Country Life in America* magazine in May of 1914.

> In going about among the shops one is impressed by the quantity of wicker furniture on display everywhere, and particularly by the great variety of designs and the number of different weaves . . . this indication of the rapidly growing popularity of wicker is easily accounted for by the fact that the public has come to consider it as a legitimate article of interior decoration rather than as a makeshift for porch and lawn use during the summer seasons . . . the manufacturer, anticipating this increase in favor, has evolved furniture of such excellence in design and construction as has never before been thought of in this kind of work; articles for everyday use that compel one's admiration and intrigue one's desire . . . from the decorative viewpoint, the chairs particularly rank very high since they are the one modern manufacture that harmonizes well with any type of antique furniture. Perhaps this is because wickerwork is older than history itself. Whatever the reason, a wicker chair will find an agreeable niche for itself in any setting and often proves a softening leaven in a group of forbidding looking Ancients!

In 1919 Heywood Brothers and Wakefield Company was the sole manufacturer of Perfek'tone wicker phonograph cabinets. These unique phonographs were advertised as the most advanced music machines ever produced, for the cabinets were handmade with reed . . . "and being non-resonant, the quality of the music issuing from the machine in the cabinet is not affected. On the other hand, the resonance of wood permits conflicting sounds to interfere with a pure reproduction." Four pages (Ills. 79–82) from the 1919 Perfek'tone catalog of wicker phonographs give us a thorough description of this unusual wicker piece that is very seldom seen today.

In the early 1900s wicker furniture was designed to be made with open latticework, to lessen the cost of labor. Thus the costly, closely woven "Cape Cod" furniture gave way to cheaper open-weave willow pieces that came to be known as "Bar Harbor" wicker (Ill. 83). Then, in 1904, public demand for lower priced, closely woven wicker furniture was answered with the advent of "fiber." Sometimes called fiber reed, or fiber rush, this highly pliable twisted paper was manmade and so inexpensive that closely woven furniture could be constructed of it very reasonably. The twisted paper was treated with a glue size, which stiffened it and helped preserve the shape of the furniture. Perhaps the most popular feature of wicker furniture made of the new fiber material was its resistance to breakage—it would not break as readily as reed or rattan. Still, reed was used far more than fiber in the making of pre-1920 wicker furniture.

In 1906 Marshall B. Lloyd, a well-known inventor and manufacturer of wicker baby buggies, moved his plant to Menominee, Michigan, and

Perfektone,

The Perfek'tone Reproducer is made to match with scientific exactness the perfect construction of the human organs of sound.

The effect of the Perfek'tone Reproducer is such that even the untrained ear can appreciate the purity of tone. The elimination of all metallic and mechanical sounds means that the greatest barrier to the successful reproduction of sound has been overcome.

The Horn, or tone amplifier, is of special design and construction. It is composed of a matrix of wood and fabric having a peculiar vibratory action of its own, and gives a fullness and sweetness of tone which can be compared to a rare old violin. Violins made of this material reproduce the tones of very old and seasoned wood.

The Perfek'tone Cabinet is the last word in acoustical science as applied to sound-reproducing instruments, having no confined air spaces or cavities to destroy the original coloring of the music. The counter vibrations, so noticeable with wood cabinets, are entirely eliminated by the use of reed and cane.

These three things control the perfect reproduction of the music. They are contained in all Perfek'tone instruments, making the quality and tone of the music the same, irrespective of the size and shape of the cabinet.

Perfektone,

STYLE No. 8, $400—OLD IVORY OR VERD MAHOGANY AND OTHER COLORS WITHOUT EXTRA CHARGE. HEAVY DUTY, TRIPLE SPRING MOTOR. ELECTRICALLY DRIVEN, $50 EXTRA. METAL PARTS GOLD, SILVER OR NICKEL-PLATED. SIZE 50 INCHES HIGH—21 INCHES WIDE—23 INCHES DEEP.

PLAYS   ALL   RECORDS

79   Page from the 1919 Perfek'tone catalog of wicker phonographs. *Wakefield Historical Society*

80   Page from the 1919 Perfek'tone catalog of wicker phonographs. *Wakefield Historical Society*

formed the Lloyd Manufacturing Company. More than a decade later, in 1917, Lloyd invented a machine to weave wicker furniture (Ill. 84), and this invention changed the face of the industry overnight. From earliest times wicker articles had been woven by hand, and although many nineteenth-century inventors (among them Cyrus Wakefield and Levi Heywood) had tried to invent a machine that could weave the material onto a frame, none had met with success. Marshall Lloyd finally succeeded by using his imagination to develop a totally new method of construction. This new method, whereby the material was woven on a loom and the frames were built according to patterns, both independently, was at the same time simple and amazing. When both the weaving and the wooden frame were completed, the woven material was carefully fitted over the framework.

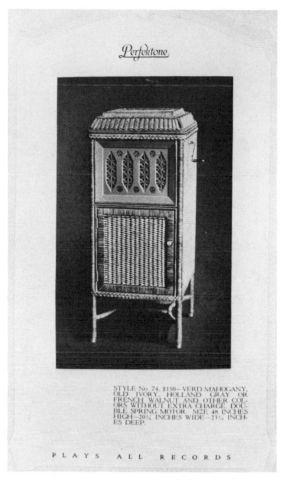

Perfektone

Perfektone

STYLE No. 74. $150—VERD MAHOGANY, OLD IVORY, HOLLAND GRAY OR FRENCH WALNUT AND OTHER COL-ORS WITHOUT EXTRA CHARGE. DOU-BLE SPRING MOTOR. SIZE 48 INCHES HIGH—20¼ INCHES WIDE—23½ INCH-ES DEEP.

PLAYS ALL RECORDS

STYLE No. 67½. $115—VERD MAHOG-ANY, OLD IVORY, HOLLAND GRAY, FRENCH WALNUT AND OTHER COL-ORS WITHOUT EXTRA CHARGE. DOU-BLE SPRING MOTOR. PLAYS FOUR 10-INCH RECORDS WITH ONE WINDING. SIZE 47 INCHES HIGH—19½ INCHES WIDE—22½ INCHES DEEP.

PLAYS ALL RECORDS

81 Page from the 1919 Perfek'tone catalog of wicker phonographs. *Wakefield Historical Society*

82 Page from the 1919 Perfek'tone catalog of wicker phonographs. *Wakefield Historical Society*

Because of its great flexibility and lower cost, Lloyd used fiber as the weaving material. He quickly became one of the largest producers of wicker baby buggies in America.

In the years following the patenting of his loom in 1917, Marshall Lloyd branched out into the competitive field of wicker furniture. Recognizing that the public had preferred the closely woven style of wicker since 1910, he began to mass-produce machine-made wicker furniture of this type to please the public taste (Ill. 85). At first, many of the established manufacturers of wicker furniture tried to compete with Lloyd Manufacturing Company by producing closely woven furniture themselves, but they soon found that, because of the cost of labor and the great amount of time involved in producing this type of wicker by hand, it was not a very profit-

83   A Bar Harbor wicker rocker. Manufacturers used this open-work weaving technique to cut down the cost of labor and material.

84   In 1917 the flat fabric loom (or Lloyd loom, as it came to be called) revolution-ized the wicker furniture industry. *A Completed Century* (1926)

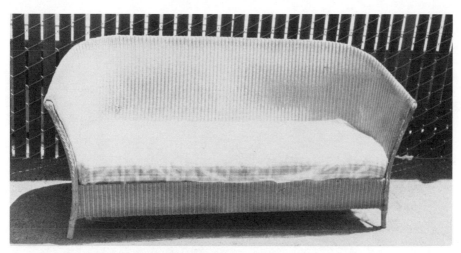

85 A machine-made wicker couch. The invention of the Lloyd loom cut down the cost of labor by mass-producing the closely woven wicker designs that were in great demand. *Al Carpenter*

able business—not in competition with the Lloyd loom, which was capable of performing the work of thirty men! Thus, Lloyd all but cornered the market on the popular closely woven wicker from 1917 until 1921, when his company was bought out and became a wholly owned subsidiary of Heywood-Wakefield Company (a simplification of the company's corporate title, which coincided with the purchase of Lloyd Manufacturing Company).

In purchasing Lloyd's company, Heywood-Wakefield Company showed that they were fully aware of the challenges of the industry and had accepted the forms and materials of mass production. It was a wise move on the part of Heywood-Wakefield, for they now owned the Lloyd loom patent, and they knew that in the years ahead there would be far greater use of fiber as the material for machine-woven furniture. Indeed, in 1912 only 15 percent of all wicker furniture was made of fiber, but by 1920 this figure had risen to almost 50 percent; by the late 1920s fiber was used in the production of 80 percent of all the wicker furniture made in America.

During the 1920s the wicker furniture industry made use of Art Deco design principles. Art Deco was a movement that completely rejected Victorian and Art Nouveau styles and replaced them with rationalism and the lessons of mass production. The new Art Deco wicker was functional and possessed a general harmony of design, yet many of the chairs and settees relied on removable inner-spring seats for comfort rather than on wickerwork (Ill. 86). The famous diamond design (Ill. 87) woven into the backs of most Art Deco wicker has become one of the key points to look for when identifying wicker furniture from the 1920s.

86 This page from the 1923 Sears, Roebuck and Company catalog clearly illustrates the popularity of upholstered wicker in the mid-twenties. G. W. Randall and Company of Michigan manufactured wicker furniture for Sears, Roebuck and Company from 1890 through the 1920s. *Sears, Roebuck and Co.*

87 The popular diamond design was sometimes painted a darker color to make it stand out, as on some of these 1920 pieces *(left)* from the Heywood-Wakefield salesroom in Chicago. *A Completed Century* (1926)

Late in that decade wicker furniture quickly began to lose its long-held popularity with the public. The manufacturers felt the decline in sales and were forced to step up their advertising campaigns, sometimes using elaborate artwork (Ill. 88), but they soon realized their efforts were to no avail. The end was clearly in sight.

I feel that two major factors led to the downfall of the wicker furniture industry in the early 1930s, and they went hand in hand: the Lloyd loom and Art Deco. With the advent of machine-made closely woven wicker there was an initial surge of popularity, but after a few years the public slowly began to feel that true craftsmanship had vanished from the wicker furniture industry. Perhaps the strongest tie between this furniture and the American public (since Cyrus Wakefield achieved his first wicker chair in the 1840s) had always been the fact that it was handmade. Moreover, the Art Deco style, which readily accepted the role of the machine and mass production, only added to public discontent.

To be sure, the true "art" of wicker furniture *was* lost in the transition from highly skilled craftsmen using their hands to produce unbelievably ornate designs with two, three, and sometimes four different types of natural material, to the use of a machine that could weave only the most basic of designs and was limited to the use of manmade fiber. Probably the last wicker designs to gain wide public acceptance before the downfall of the industry are those shown in the 1927 Heywood-Wakefield Company trade catalogs. Illustrations 89 through 94 reproduce a half-dozen pages from that catalog. Following these catalog pages are 21 photographs showing fine pieces of wicker furniture dating from the turn of the century to the late 1920s.

Heywood - Wakefield reed and fibre furniture will bring charm, color, and comfort to your home. This artistic furniture, with its beautiful upholsteries and sparkling color combinations, has a well deserved place in every interior decorative scheme. It is the furniture of today — reflecting the colorful and comfortable trend in modern arts and decoration. With no other type of furniture can you express your individuality in the home as with Heywood-Wakefield reed and fibre, because in texture, design, and colorings it is truly different. ❧ There is a wide variety of complete suites and individual pieces, including occasional chairs, end tables, ferneries, writing desks, tea wagons, lamps, fireside seats, etc. ❧ The prices are reasonable and the quality is high, which means that for a small sum you can have in your home beautiful, comfortable, modern furniture that will give exceptionally long and satisfying service. Your dealer will be glad to show you the new suites and single pieces.

Fibre Chair, R 678 C, and End Table, R 672 G, are illustrated.

Send 6 cents to Heywood-Wakefield Company, 209 Washington Street, Boston, Mass., to cover the cost of mailing our "Color Furniture in the Home", a 52-page booklet on interior decoration.

HEYWOOD~WAKEFIELD

88   One ot Heywood-Wakefield's unique advertisements to boost sales in the late twenties. *Reprinted with permission from "The Saturday Evening Post"* © 1928; The Curtis Publishing Company

89   Wicker rockers, armchairs, and settees from the 1927 Heywood-Wakefield catalog. *Wakefield Historical Society*

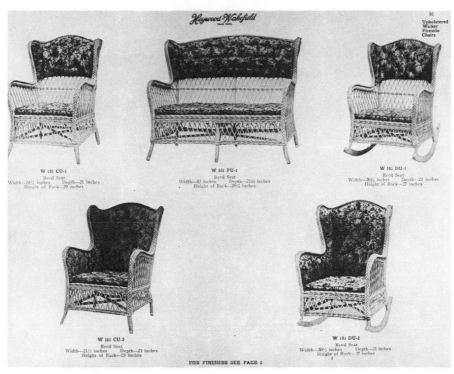

90   Wicker armchairs and rockers from the 1927 Heywood-Wakefield catalog.
Wakefield Historical Society

91   Various wicker pieces from the 1927 Heywood-Wakefield catalog. *Wakefield Historical Society*

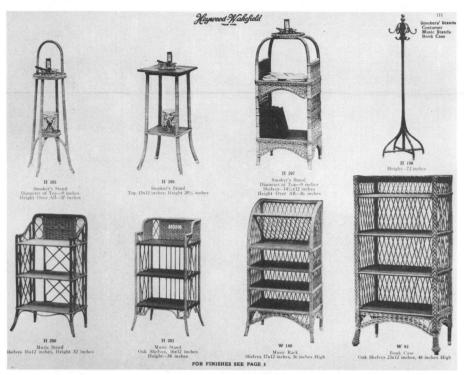

92   Wicker couches from the 1927 Heywood-Wakefield catalog. *Wakefield Historical Society*

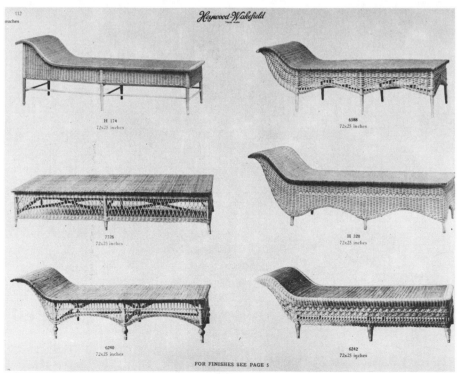

93 Wicker lamps from the 1927 Heywood-Wakefield catalog. *Wakefield Historical Society*

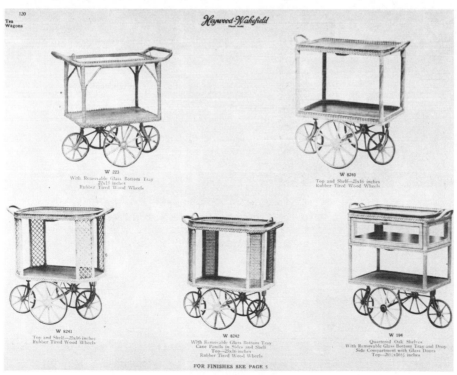

94 Wicker tea carts from the 1927 Heywood-Wakefield catalog. *Wakefield Historical Society*

95   Two examples of wicker rockers from the twenties. LEFT: Machine-made upholstered rocker made of fiber. RIGHT: The popular Bar Harbor wicker rocker made of reed. *John Hathaway*

96 TOP: The hourglass design of this rattan chair goes back to seventeenth-century China. This particular style of hourglass chair was being manufactured in the twenties and is still on the market today. BOTTOM LEFT: Wood and reed armchair from the turn of the century. BOTTOM RIGHT: Wicker desk chair.

97   Four examples of wicker armchairs from the twenties. TOP LEFT: A wing-back chair with magazine-rack side pockets. TOP RIGHT: Bar Harbor armchair. BOTTOM LEFT: Tightly woven wicker chair. BOTTOM RIGHT: Wicker chair with upholstered seat.

98 Three styles of wicker lounges. TOP: Bar Harbor–style lounge. BOT-TOM LEFT: Upholstered lounge with magazine-rack side pockets. *Beverly Stephenson.* BOTTOM RIGHT: Upholstered, tightly woven lounge with open back.

99   Two wicker desks from the twenties. *Frank Stagg (top)*

100 Various styles of wicker lamps. *Frank Stagg*

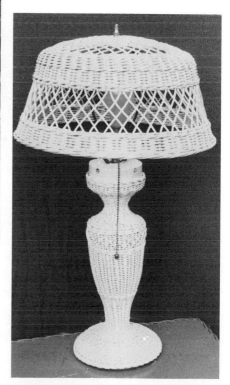

101   Two bookcases. *Frank Stagg (right);*
Beverly Stephenson (below)

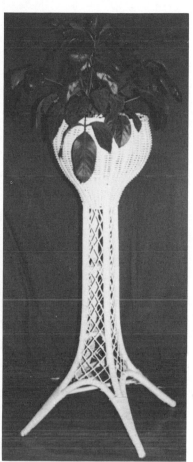

102 Plant stands. TOP LEFT: Unique Art Nouveau double planter with birdcage. *Frank Stagg.* TOP RIGHT: Tall fernery. BOTTOM LEFT: Common rectangular plant stand with metal liner. BOTTOM RIGHT: Combination fernery and birdcage.

103   TOP: Coffee table with glass top. *Frank Stagg.* BOTTOM
LEFT: Oak gateleg table. *Frank Stagg.* BOTTOM RIGHT:
Small bedside table.

104   Two wicker tea carts. *Frank Stagg (top)*

105   Rare wicker picture frames. *Frank Stagg*

106 Children's wicker from the twenties. TOP: Wicker doll bed, doll's high chair, and child's rocker. BOTTOM LEFT: Child's rocker. BOTTOM RIGHT: Buggy with adjustable hood.

107   Wicker porch swings. TOP: Swing from the twenties, made of fiber, and about seven feet in length. BOTTOM: Basket swing, c. 1914.

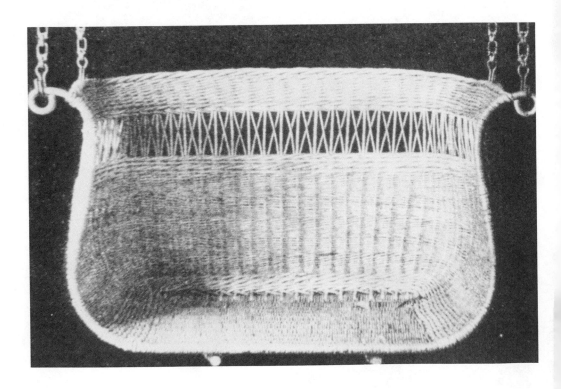

109 Wicker hat rack
     or clothes tree.

108 Round wicker table and four matching straight-back chairs.
     Gloria Muzio

110 Tightly woven wicker bed frame. *Frank Slagg*

111 Cushioned round wicker bench with
     umbrella top made of bamboo. Very
     rare.

RESTORING WICKER FURNITURE

WHY RESTORE ANTIQUE WICKER?

The restoration of antique wicker furniture has long been considered a lost art. Many people seem to think that once wicker is damaged, they cannot do anything about it. Nothing could be further from the truth. All wicker furniture can be restored in one degree or another, and usually there is a good chance of complete restoration unless the framework has rotted over the years. However, why restore antique wicker when reproductions of fancy Victorian wicker furniture are available at lower prices?

The answer is that antique wicker is far more durable, in both structure and design, than the wicker reproductions being made today. The quality of the materials employed in both the framework and the weaving is far superior to that of the materials from which modern reproductions are made. There is also the fact that a truly old piece of wicker furniture is considered an antique, and any antique is worth restoring to its original state. One must take into consideration as well that the value of antique wicker in good condition is climbing at such an alarming rate that this furniture should be looked on as an investment, as well as beautiful and useful to own.

MATERIALS

Just as different types of materials were used in making wicker furniture (see Chapter 1), these materials themselves also came in various sizes and shapes. The Appendix following this chapter provides a list of the craft supply houses in the United States that carry wickerwork materials of all kinds. The best procedure is to write one of these companies and either ask for a price list of the wickerwork materials they have in stock, or simply send them a small sample of the material from a damaged piece and ask them to identify it and its size and tell you the price per pound or hank.

Illustration 112 shows the most commonly used materials employed in the making of wicker furniture. The supply houses listed in the Appendix can supply all—or at least some— of these materials.

| 1 | 2 | 3 | 4 | 5 |

112 The most common materials used in restoring wicker furniture: (1) round reed, (2) flat reed, (3) binding cane, (4) fiber, (5) sea grass.

PREPARATION OF MATERIALS

Before attempting any wicker repair techniques, it is important to know that some materials must be prepared before they can be used. In the immediately following paragraphs, instructions are given for preparing reed, cane, sea grass, and fiber.

REED

Either round or flat reed should be soaked in warm water before being used. Reed is a supple material when wet, but it will snap very easily if it is worked dry. A good rule to follow is this: the thicker the reed, the longer it should be soaked. Thinner reeds need only three minutes' soaking to become supple, whereas thick round reeds should be soaked for about ten minutes. It is important to soak only the amount of reed that will be used promptly because reed frays and splits when left to soak for longer than thirty minutes.

CANE

Binding cane is used extensively in wrapping the framework of wicker furniture, but it should never be worked dry. Simply pass it through water quickly to make it supple and lessen the chances of cracking. Cane that is shipped in a coil is sometimes difficult to straighten. If such proves to be the case, the entire coil should be soaked in warm water for a few minutes, then hung on a hook to drop out straight and dry. Cane should not be stored near heaters or hot pipes, as it will become brittle and break easily.

FIBER AND SEA GRASS

Both these materials should be worked dry. They are extremely supple in their natural state, and no preparation is necessary.

TOOLS

Here are the basic tools and related supplies needed to restore wicker furniture: a hammer; ½-inch to ¾-inch nails; glue (Weldwood white glue is recommended); and a pair of sharp hand clippers or heavy scissors. An electric drill is also needed for some of the more difficult repair jobs. All tools and materials should be close at hand and arranged for convenient use. If there is one single thing that slows down the worker's progress it is taking time out to hunt for misplaced tools or materials.

TECHNIQUES OF WICKER RESTORATION

The following pages illustrate some of the more basic wicker restoration techniques that can be mastered by the layman in a short amount of time. The key word in trying your hand at some or all of these techniques is PATIENCE. If you are patient and careful with your materials, there is no reason why you cannot restore your own wicker furniture—an accomplishment that is most rewarding.

WRAPPING

113   This chair leg needs to be rewrapped with binding cane. It is far easier to turn a chair over and work on it with the leg sticking up. After removing all nails from the bare wood, nail the loose cane to the wood, making sure that the nail is facing the inside of the chair so it will not be visible from the front.

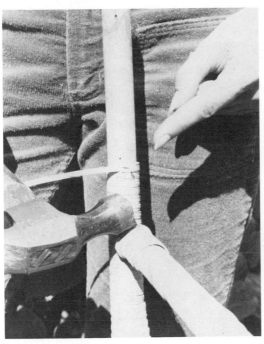

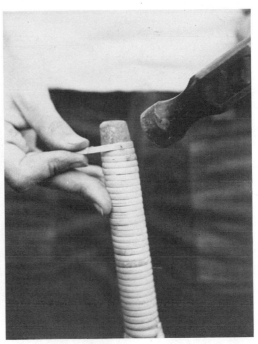

114 The new length of cane is placed over the broken cane and nailed to the leg in the same manner.

115 The binding cane is wrapped tightly around the bare leg to within a half-inch from the top. Then the same nailing procedure is used to fasten the end of it. Remember always to nail the cane on the inside so that the nail will not show when the chair is turned upright.

116 Both the top and bottom ends of the cane wrapping are cut close to the nail, and glue is spread over the freshly cut ends, next to the nails.

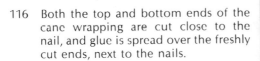

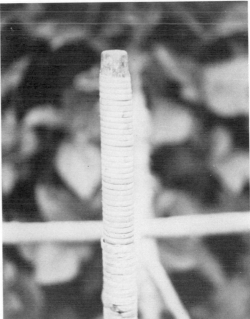

REPLACING SPOKES

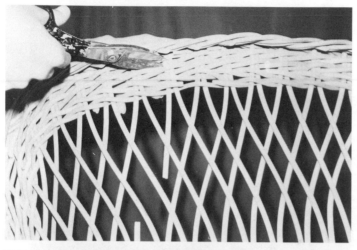

117 To replace a broken vertical reed, or "spoke," the broken reed must first be removed by snipping it off at the top, above the third or fourth row of the woven horizontal reeds.

118 The bottom of the broken spoke must then be snipped out below the fourth row of the lower woven horizontal reeds.

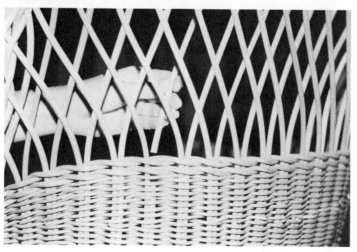

119 A new spoke is fitted into place after it has been soaked. Note that all the spokes follow a pattern: those in the front slant one way and those in the back slant in the opposite direction. It is important to determine what the original pattern was and to follow it carefully.

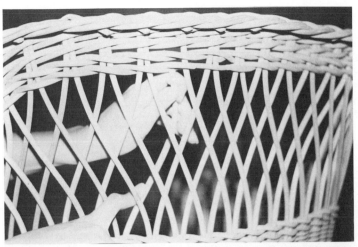

120 The new round reed spoke is inserted between the bottom rows of horizontal weaving. Then it is carefully bent in the middle so that the other end can be inserted between the weaving at the top of the chair. If the spoke does not slide through the horizontal weaving easily, don't force it—take the clippers and cut a sharp point on the tip of the spoke. This point should make it possible to push the spoke through the weaving with less resistance.

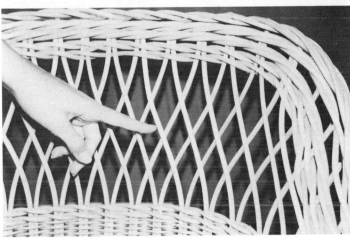

121 The end result should look like this. Gluing is not necessary in most cases.

LOCKING

122   One of the most common flaws in wicker furniture is a missing or damaged horizontal reed.

123   In order to replace a single horizontal reed, first snap the damaged reed off just under the spokes to the left and right. In this photo a screwdriver is inserted under the damaged reed and lifted up to snap off the reed directly under the spoke to the left. When it is possible to clip the horizontal reed from the back, I recommend doing so, but in this case (since the repair is on a hollow, serpentine back) a screwdriver and leverage had to be employed in snapping the reed off under the spoke.

124   Locking is the laying together of the ends of a weaving strand. The two ends of the new reed are inserted (*left* and *right*) under the cutoff ends of the old reed, thus forming a fastening.

125   The finished job is shown here. The new horizontal reed usually dries tightly into place, but glue is sometimes necessary to ensure a permanent bond.

UNDER-AND-OVER-WEAVE

126 This chair is fairly simple to repair because all the spokes are intact.

127 Don't be afraid to cut away loose or uneven reeds.

128   The under-and-over weave is simple. The first row to be re-woven should be the exact opposite of the last row above it that was left intact. In this photo, for example, the new weave is started *under* the spoke because the reed directly above it begins by going *over* the first spoke.

129   The under-and-over weave is well named, for the technique used in this weave consists of weaving under one spoke and over the next. One hand should be used as a kind of guide to feed the reed to the other hand (under the seat), which pulls the reed slowly through.

130   The end result should look like this. A light coat of white glue spread over the repaired material is recommended to both strengthen the weave and seal the reed for painting.

COMBINING TECHNIQUES

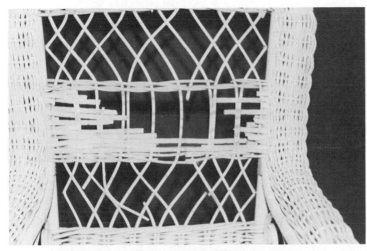

131 Before attempting to restore a piece like this one, be sure that you have mastered all the techniques illustrated up to this point. All the restoration techniques covered will be put to use on this repair job.

132 The first step is to clip out the damaged spokes.

133 After damaged spokes are removed, study the design of the spokes to make sure that the restoration job duplicates the original pattern.

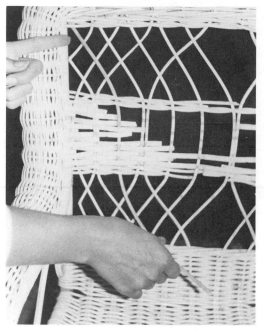

134 Soak the correct size of round reed until it is pliable. Insert the new spoke up through the weave (middle section). Remember to follow the pattern of the original spokes (leaning to the left or right), and insert the tips of the spokes about one inch into the rolled, hollow serpentine back.

135 Glue all spokes into place and let the glue set for one hour. The spokes are the skeleton of any wicker piece, and should therefore be very secure before any weaving is attempted.

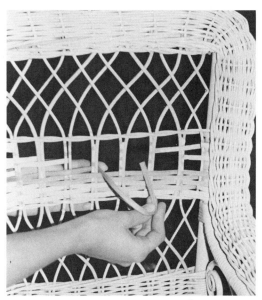

136 After the spokes are glued into place, restore the horizontal under-and-over weave in the middle section. The flat reed for this is soaked to ensure flexibility and then woven onto the skeleton of spokes. The same method of locking is put to use here: the starting end of the new reed and the cutoff end of the old reed lie close together and form a fastening.

137 The finished job is now ready for painting.

HOLLOW SERPENTINE ARMS

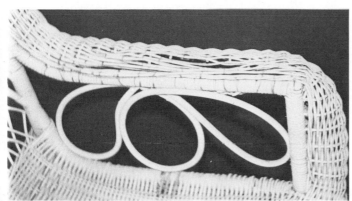

138 A caved-in hollow serpentine arm is one of the most common flaws in old wicker furniture. Although these rounded arms were beautiful to look at, they were also usually the first part of the chair to be broken—simply because the arms are major stress points. All previous restoration techniques should be completely mastered before such a job is attempted.

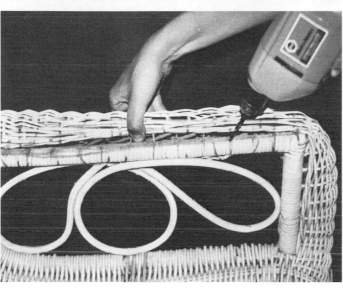

139 An electric drill should be used to make ½-inch holes in the wooden framework. The original holes (some will still have the broken spokes inside) will show you where to drill. Be careful to use the right size bit, for the holes must be large enough for the new spokes to fit into snugly. Drill holes for all the spokes that need to be replaced.

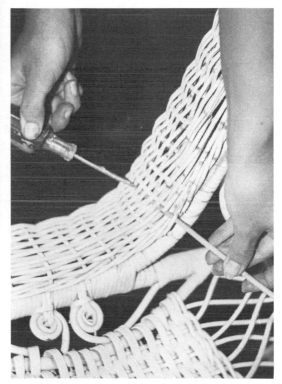

140 After soaking the correct size of round reed until it is very pliable, insert the sharpened tip of a new spoke into the weave alongside the broken spoke. Carefully push it through the weave, using a screwdriver to guide it along from the top.

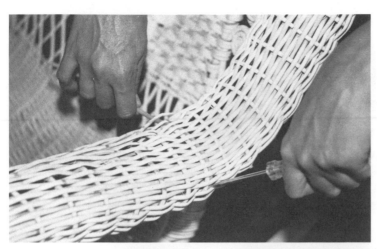

141   Continue the process described in Ill. 140 until the new spoke is pushed completely around the arm.

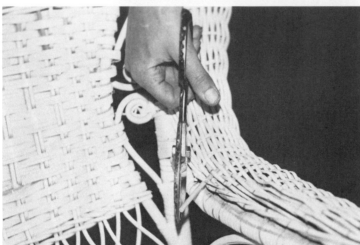

142   Now clip the other end of the new spoke at a slight angle to ensure easy insertion into the hole you have drilled for it.

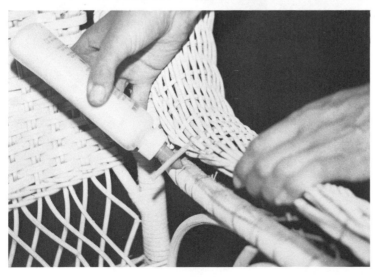

143   In order to ensure a tight bond, fill the hole with white glue before inserting the spoke.

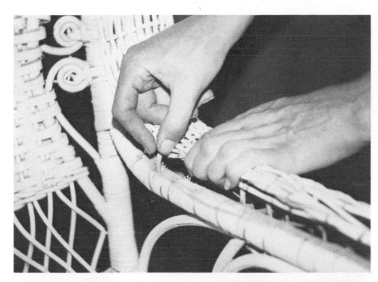

144 Carefully bend the spoke and fit it into the glue-filled hole. The spoke may have to be re-cut several times, to make it the proper length to match the height of the old spokes directly behind it. Also try to duplicate the curve of the arch of the original spokes.

145 When the new spoke has dried into place, clip off the old damaged spoke next to it and carefully pull it out.

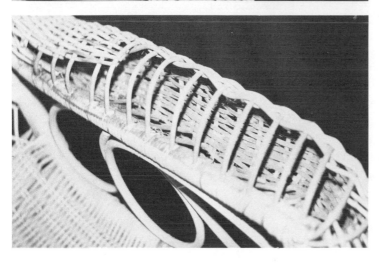

146 Repeat the steps shown in Ills. 140 to 145 until all the new spokes are in place and the glue has set. Now that the skeleton of spokes has been restored, weaving is the next step. First, however, clip the old woven horizontal reeds back so that they are all tucked *under* one of the spokes.

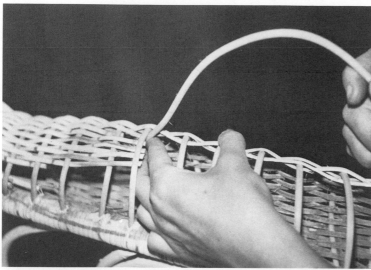

147   Start weaving by locking the new reed under both the spoke and the end of the old reed.

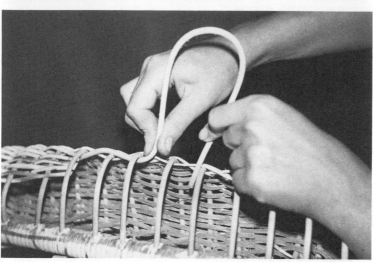

148   When weaving, be careful not to put too much pressure on any of the spokes or they may be pulled out of the framework. It is helpful to brace the reed next to the spoke with one hand while guiding the end of the reed through the spokes with the other hand.

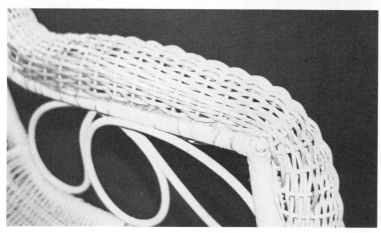

149   The finished arm should be covered with a thin coat of white glue to ensure durability as well as to seal the porous reeds.

INSTALLING A SET-IN CANE SEAT

If you are interested in restoring your old wicker chair or settee completely, it is a good idea to learn how to install a prewoven, or set-in, cane seat. Over 90 percent of all wicker furniture made with cane seats had this type of set-in seat (developed by Mr. Watkins of Heywood Brothers and Company) to save on the high labor costs of hand caning. It is easy to determine whether or not any chair once had a set-in cane seat: if a series of small holes circles the seat opening, the chair was originally caned by hand, but if a groove runs around the perimeter of the seat, you can be sure the chair originally had a set-in cane seat.

REMOVING OLD CANE AND SPLINE
The first step in replacing set-in cane seats is to be sure that the surrounding groove is clean. More often than not, you will have to remove old cane and some leftover spline (a triangular-shaped reed that fits into the groove) with a wide chisel and hammer. First, place the chisel on the inner edge of the spline and tap carefully around the entire seat with a hammer, to loosen the spline from the frame. Repeat the same procedure around the outside of the spline. After the spline is loosened, slowly lift it out with a screwdriver. Be very careful not to chip the wood around the groove.

PREPARATION AND MATERIALS
First, select spline that fits into the groove easily and can be removed with your fingers. If the spline does not fit into the groove smoothly, it will be too large when it dries. The seat used here as an example has rounded corners, but some seats have square or mitered corners, and for these seats the spline should be installed in cut lengths.

Next, the prewoven cane itself should be soaked in warm water for two to three hours to make it pliable, and then hung on a hook for five minutes to drip dry. The spline should also be soaked, but for only fifteen minutes (just before starting work).

You will also need two wooden wedges—one with a sharp point to drive the cane into the groove, the other with a blunt end to hammer the spline into the groove without damaging the spline itself. Soft wood is best to use if you are making these wedges yourself; hard wood can break the cane. (Wooden wedges, as well as the prewoven cane and the spline, can be ordered at some or all of the supply houses listed in the Appendix.)

The following tools and related items are also necessary: a hammer, a mat knife, clippers, and white glue (Weldwood or LePage's Original glue recommended).

If you follow the illustrated step-by-step instructions, you should be able to install your own set-in cane seat:

INSTALLING A SET-IN CANE SEAT

150   Be sure that all old cane, spline, and hardened glue are removed from the groove. The paragraphs preceding these illustrations contain instructions on how to do this.

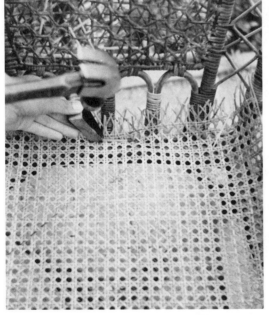

151   After the cane webbing has been soaked, place it over the seat with the glossy side up. Then, with the sharp-pointed wooden wedge, lightly tap a few inches of the cane into the groove at the back of the chair. Next, cut a temporary wedge of spline (about one inch in length) and drive it over the depressed cane and into the groove with the blunt-end wooden wedge. This piece of spline will serve as a temporary holding device. Repeat the same procedure at the front of the chair, so that the cane is pulled tight from the front to the back of the seat.

152   After the two spline wedges are in place, take the sharp wooden wedge and—with a hammer—carefully tap down the cane webbing into the groove all around the seat until the outline of the groove can be seen clearly.

153 Remove the two small spline wedges from the front and back of the seat, and pour a small amount of white glue around the path of the groove. Now, using the blunt-end wooden wedge and the presoaked spline, begin to tap the spline into the groove.

154 After the spline has been lightly hammered into the groove all around the seat, cut the end of it very carefully so that it will butt up against the other end of the spline at the back of the seat.

155 When the entire length of spline has been inserted into the groove, use the mat knife to cut off the excess strands of cane around the outside. Take great care not to slice into the spline with the mat knife.

156 After the excess cane has been completely removed, go around the seat again with the blunt-end wedge and a hammer, pounding the spline into the groove until it is level with the wooden seat frame. Finally, pour glue along the length of the spline, and work it in on both sides, to ensure a tight bond. (Excess glue can be removed with a wet cloth.) Let the chair dry at normal room temperature for two days before you use it. Do *not* set it outdoors in the sun to dry.

CARE OF WICKER

CLEANING WICKER FURNITURE

The best method of cleaning wicker furniture is to go over it thoroughly with a soft brush and warm soapy water. A toothbrush is recommended for hard-to-get-at places. Wicker pieces made of reed and willow (both natural and painted) should be periodically wiped off with a soft wet cloth. If this type of wicker becomes brittle, it should be taken outside and hosed off—the water will feed the reeds and ensure greater flexibility. On the other hand, a piece of wicker made of either fiber (twisted paper) or sea grass should never be hosed off because water will weaken the weave as well as the individual fibers. To clean this type of wicker furniture use a damp cloth only.

Very diluted domestic bleach will whiten soiled reed and willow pieces that have been left in their natural state, but this procedure should be used with great caution and only if scrubbing with warm soapy water does not do the job.

PRESERVING NATURAL WICKER

In referring to wicker furniture, the term "natural" designates any piece left unpainted. Originally, all the so-called natural wicker was actually either stained or coated with a protective coat of clear varnish or lacquer. Natural wicker should be left unpainted whenever possible because it is far more valuable than painted wicker; it will also withstand the weather better if used outdoors.

After cleaning natural wicker, you can maintain its natural light beige color by applying a coat of colorless lacquer to protect it from soil and wear. A thin solution of an acrylic resin (such as a polyurethane type of varnish) will also give the surface of natural wicker a protective skin that will resist soiling.

STRIPPING PAINTED WICKER

Many people wonder if painted wicker can be stripped back to its natural state. The answer is yes—but with some reservations. Most wicker furniture made of reed, rattan, and willow can be successfully stripped of paint by a reliable professional furniture stripper. One key to success, however, is making sure the material is not manmade fiber, for the chemicals in the stripper's "hot tank" will eat through that material in no time at all. By contrast, most other types of wicker furniture can be stripped of a dozen or more layers of paint without suffering permanent damage. The chemicals in the hot tank will sometimes raise small, whiskerlike fibers from the individual reeds, but these are easy to deal with. The most efficient way of removing them is to singe off all the affected areas with a propane torch set at a low flame. Remember, always, that after wicker furniture has been stripped and allowed to dry out, to ensure flexibility it must be sealed, stained, varnished, or otherwise treated.

REFINISHING NATURAL WICKER

Whether staining an entire wicker chair or merely staining a small repair job to match the existing finish, it is a wise first step to secure from your local hardware or paint dealer a booklet illustrating the use of stains and dyes on various materials. Because it is important to stain a piece with a substance that is compatible with the original finish, it is always a good idea to try a little of any new stain on a hidden area. Then wait for results before going ahead with the entire job. Sometimes different stains react against each other and cracks or blisters develop. Even if this does happen, the piece will not be ruined if the test was made in a hidden area. Should the first stain prove incompatible, test another one that has a different chemical base. When you have found a stain that is compatible with the original, apply several thin coats, slowly darkening the stain with each application until the desired depth of color is obtained.

Because of its porosity, wicker furniture soils very easily unless some type of clear finish is used as a sealer. The best way to do this is to apply two or three light coats of a good grade varnish. Spray finishing, using either a commercial aerosol can or a compressor, is the best method of evenly distributing a varnish, shellac, or clear lacquer finish on wicker furniture.

PAINTING WICKER

Most antique wicker furniture has been painted one color or another—white and some shade of green or brown were among the favorite colors of years past. Today many people still paint wicker furniture because of personal preference or to match the color of a specific room. Regardless of your reasons, if you decide to paint your wicker, do so with care and only after reading this section.

Cleaning and preparation are the key elements in doing a successful paint job on wicker furniture. All dirt and dust should be removed from the piece before painting begins (see "Cleaning Wicker Furniture"). When the existing paint is chipped or flaking, try to remove any loose flakes with a wire brush. If this does not work—and sometimes it doesn't—it may be necessary to send the piece to a professional stripper to have all the old paint removed so that there is a smooth surface to paint on (see "Stripping Painted Wicker," for precautions). Some of the older pieces, especially those that were used outdoors, were painted every year. Since this annual summer ritual of painting was fairly common in the past, some old wicker bears virtually dozens of coats of globbed-on paint. The only way to remove such a buildup of paint, with the attendant drippings and thick puddlings that have accumulated and dried over the years, is to have the piece professionally stripped.

It is extremely difficult—sometimes impossible—to paint wicker successfully with a brush, and so I strongly recommend spray painting. If you are doing only one or two small pieces, I suggest using a high-grade commercial spray paint in an aerosol can (gloss lacquer or enamel) in order to cut costs. It is especially important, when using canned spray paint, to get a strong, steady spray. The best way to ensure this is to (1) shake the can vigorously for three or four minutes before using and (2) keep the spray nozzle clean of any paint buildup (use a pin to unclog the hole).

When painting more than just a couple of pieces of wicker, however, I recommend using a compressor for a professional-quality job. Although it takes more time to use a compressor, and the cost is significantly higher than for using a spray can, the results are truly worth the extra effort and expense if you want a long-lasting, high-quality job. For the compressor paint job, get a high-grade acrylic enamel automotive paint (Sherwin-Williams is recommended) and an enamel reducing compound to thin it out (three parts enamel to one part reducer).

Regardless of which method of spray painting you choose, the actual painting should be done outdoors in dry, warm weather. It is best to spray the underside of a piece first, then turn it right side up to complete the job. The most important rules in spray painting wicker furniture are these: (1) Use several thin coats rather than a single heavy one; (2) allow each coat to dry completely before applying the next one. Remember, there is far less chance for unsightly drips to accumulate if you follow these simple rules.

WHAT TO LOOK FOR WHEN BUYING OLD WICKER FURNITURE

The first thing to determine when buying wicker furniture is its age. Naturally, the older the piece is, the more valuable it is to the collector or antique dealer. One of the main problems I have run across in restoring wicker furniture for the public is the general confusion in identifying old wicker and spotting reproductions. Some reproductions from the Far East can be a problem because the designs are usually Victorian in nature, with flowing lines and curlicues. There are, however, a few key points to look for if you are not sure whether a piece is old or a reproduction. The seats on reproduction wicker chairs are never cane seats with wooden frames, but rather flimsy, circular-woven reed seats. These seats are usually a dead giveaway, and more often than not they are damaged because of their poor construction. Reproductions are also much lighter than old wicker pieces because the framework is made of bamboo rather than wood. Another clue is the poor quality of the reeds used in reproductions—they are fibrous and usually very brittle.

The next thing to consider is the condition of the piece. As I have demonstrated in this chapter, almost any damage to the wickerwork itself can be restored. The framework, however, presents a different problem, so examine it with extra care. Many older pieces have been left outdoors for years and the framework has warped or, in some extreme cases, been rotted by the elements. Most structural damage (such as loose dowels) can easily be repaired, but any weak joints that lie hidden under the wickerwork usually entail removal of the wicker around the joint, repairing the joint, and then restoring the wickerwork to its original condition. This long process usually requires a professional repairman and can be quite costly.

For the beginning collector, the best wicker furniture to invest in is basic pieces such as rockers, armchairs, settees, lounges, and plant stands. The more specialized pieces—baby carriages, for example—are sometimes worth more money, but reselling them may present a problem simply because something like a rocker will appeal to more buyers than a baby carriage will.

The price one must pay for antique wicker furniture is often affected by geographic location. Usually prices are somewhat higher in the larger cities. The following list provides current price ranges for some of the more popular pieces, in good condition   even a rare piece may be a questionable investment if it is in very poor condition. These, of course, are average price ranges. Remember always that age, condition, finish, and design must also be taken into consideration.

Wicker from the Victorian Era

Rocker	$100–$275
Platform rocker	$200–$300
Settee	$175–$350
Armchair	$100–$225
Fernery	$ 50–$125
Corner chair	$125–$300
Conversation chair	$200–$350
Lounge	$150–$350
Baby carriage	$150–$300
Sewing basket	$ 75–$125

Wicker from 1900 to 1930

Rocker	$ 75–$175
Armchair	$ 75–$150
Settee	$125–$250
Rectangular plant stand	$ 35–$ 65
Porch swing	$200–$375
Lounge	$100–$225
Round dining room table	$150–$250 (more with an oak top)
Baby carriage	$ 75–$175
Phonograph cabinet	$250–$500 (depending on condition of the machine)
Set of four dining chairs	$150–$275
Floor lamp	$125–$300
Table lamp	$125–$250

APPENDIX

Minor American Manufacturers of Wicker Furniture

The following list of minor American wicker manufacturers (the major manufacturers have already been mentioned at length in the text) does not pretend to be complete; it is simply a listing of the company labels I have come across over the years in the course of my repair work.

Many firms did not label their furniture at all. Some of the companies listed here were in existence for only a short time, but I have included them anyhow, for the benefit of readers who may come upon pieces bearing such a label.

American Fiber Company (Sheboygan, Wis.)
The Bolton Willow Shop (Cambridge, Mass.)
Boston Willow Furniture Company (Boston, Mass.)
Bielecky Brothers, Inc. (New York, N.Y.)
A. Cummings (New York, N.Y.)
Cunningham Reed and Rattan Company (New York, N.Y.)
F. Debski (New York, N.Y.)
Ficks Reed Company (New York, N.Y.); established 1928
Heywood-Morrill (Gardner, Mass.) 1870s–97
Jenkins-Phipps (Wakefield, Mass.) 1905–12
Jones-Smith (New York, N.Y.)
The Larkin Company (Buffalo, N.Y.)
Leader

McGibbon & Company (New York, N.Y.)
Joseph P. McHugh & Son (New York, N.Y.); established 1878
Mentzer Reed Company (Grand Rapids, Mich.)
Minnet & Company
Novelty Rattan Company (Boston, Mass.)
Paine's Furniture Company
Peabody & Whitney
Pioneer
The Reed Shop
The Bemis Riddell Fiber Company (Sheboygan, Wis.)
Stickley-Brandt Furniture Company (Binghamton, N.Y.)
John Wanamaker (Philadelphia, Penn.)

Craft Supply Houses

The following list includes some of the craft supply houses in the United States that carry wickerwork materials (reed, rattan, cane, fiber, and so on) for do-it-yourself wicker furniture restoration:

Bersted's Hobby Craft, Inc.
521 W. 10th Ave.
P.O. Box 40
Monmouth, Ill. 61462

Dick Blick Company
P.O. Box 1267
Galesburg, Ill. 61401

Boin Arts & Crafts Company
87 Morris St.
Morristown, N.J. 07960

Cane & Basket Supply Company
1283 South Cochran Ave.
Los Angeles, Calif. 90019

Earth Guild/Grateful Union
Mail Order Service Dept.
15 Tudor St.
Cambridge, Mass. 02139

The Handcrafters
1 West Brown St.
Waupon, Wis. 53963

The Hidden Village
215 Yale Ave.
Claremont, Calif. 91711

Macmillan Arts & Crafts, Inc.
9520 Baltimore Ave.
College Park, Md. 20740

Maid of Scandinavia Company
3244 Raleigh Ave.
Minneapolis, Minn. 55416

Nasco Handcrafters
901 Janesville Ave.
Fort Atkinson, Wis. 53538

Note: Nasco has a second location at
1524 Princeton Ave.
Modesto, Calif. 95352

Naturalcraft
2199 Bancroft Way
Berkeley, Calif. 94704

Peerless Rattan & Reed Mfg. Co. Inc.
97 Washington St.
New York, N.Y. 10006

Riley Street Annex
630 Fifth St.
Santa Rosa, Calif. 95404

Savin Handcrafts
P.O. Box 4251
Hamden, Conn. 06514

Sax Arts & Crafts
P.O. Box 2002
Milwaukee, Wis. 53201

The Sheep Village
2005 Bridgeway
Sausalito, Calif. 94965

Straw Into Gold
P.O. Box 2904
5509 College Ave.
Oakland, Calif. 94618

INDEX